Action Stations

To all shipmates, past and present

Action Stations

COLIN REID

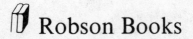 Robson Books

First published in Great Britain in 1987 by Robson Books Ltd.,
Bolsover House, 5-6 Clipstone Street, London WIP 7EB

British Library Cataloguing in Publication Data

Reid, Colin
    History of Broadcasting House.
    1. British Broadcasting Corporation
    2. Celebrities
    1. Title
    384.54′092′2   PN1990.6.G7

ISBN 0-86051-425-0

Typesetting by AKM Associates (UK) Ltd
Ajmal House, Hayes Road, Southall, London

Printed and bound in Great Britain by
Biddles Ltd, Guildford and King's Lynn

Contents

ACKNOWLEDGMENTS

In the compilation of this book, I particularly wish to thank the following shipmates:

Mrs Jacqueline Kavanagh and Mr John Jordan for their excellent service at the BBC Written Archives Centre at Caversham; likewise Mr David Evans and his staff at the Radio Reference Library; Central Services Division at Broadcasting House; Mr Cecil Madden, who generously allowed me to survey his own treasure-chest; Mr Roger Pearce, a doughty colleague in the Purser's Office, who rendered me valuable assistance with the Ship's Log; Mr Freddie Hill and Staff of BBC Welfare Department, who helped me to find old-stagers; and all those who willingly related their personal anecdotes.

My thanks are also due to Diane and Jean Leonard for their help with stenography, to Peter Agland for his assistance with photography and to Tony Matthews for his cartoons.

CR., 1987

Preface

TO THE COUNTLESS MEMBERS of BBC crews and broadcasters
that I have not mentioned in this book, I offer my apologies. I
am well aware that many deserving names are missing from the
Passenger List on the fifty-five year voyage. Space has not
permitted me to include you all. Primarily, it is the 'ship', the
steel battleship, on whose decks you have all served that carries
star billing, supported by a cast of Cecil B. de Mille proportions.
The scenario stretches from Savoy Hill to the Satellites.

List of Illustrations

Foreword

THE NEW HEADQUARTERS AT Portland Place brought about a sudden change of atmosphere as well as activity. What somebody said about 'BH', as it has always been called, is that when he went in and went up to the desk he always felt as if he ought to ask for a towel as well as a bathing-dress, because there's something very open and something very austere about the building, and one felt rather cowed with the solemn notice about Reith at the top, and commissionaires all over the place, and the huge desk that makes a good first impression. True, they'd put Eril Gill's 'Prospero and Ariel' over those massive swing-doors, as a civilized gesture, and there were window-boxes outside the third-floor Council Chamber, but there is all that echoing stone and marble. Yes, one saw where the towel came in.

The Latin phrase carved underneath Eric Gill's statue of a Sower in the entrance hall is 'DEUS INCREMENTUM DAT' – to the staff a perpetual reminder that a rise in salary came from God alone!

In many ways it was a great improvement on Savoy Hill though it lost a lot of the character by the division made in the new building between staff and artists. The staff lifts were in the main hall and the artists' lifts were behind them through a doorway. It was a change from the character of Savoy Hill, where studios and offices were all mixed up together and you would frequently find members of office staff in the passages talking to artists; a lot of the 'chumminess' disappeared. The idea of separate lifts for staff and artists soon broke down and they became just lifts for anybody to use, which usually meant the nearest one to their office.

The Director-General (Sir John Reith), Senior Controllers, Chief Engineer and the Accountant were all housed in the nose of the building on the third floor. The Director-General's office was the largest in the building, as would befit his status and also his stature which was well over six feet, and it was the only office which had a fireplace. Whether it was because he'd specifically asked to see *you*, or whether it was a courtesy gesture, if you were summoned to see him you had three thoughts in your mind: was it the sack; was it promotion; or was it the quality of your work in which he had an interest? To get into his office on the third floor you walked through a fairly large ante-room before being ushered in to the great man; you had to walk at least twenty paces to get to his desk, which was also a very large affair. You were always asked to sit down while he stood up and walked round the room making his comments; he was very impressive, like a headmaster in the big school. The DG's meeting with you was quite clearly at an end when he indicated as such, and one came away either with deep depression or pleasure if it meant anything like promotion.

He had of course absolute power over the whole staff from the junior office boy to the Senior Controller. The remaining senior officers of the BBC were grouped around this office, all of which being in the nose of the building looked straight down past All Souls, Langham Place, and down Regent Street. They were clustered in these offices like bees around a Queen bee. Status was marked by having curtains in your office, a carpet on the floor instead of linoleum and a key for the use of one of the private lavatories. The highest status ever reached was during the War, when Sir Basil Nicolls became Senior Controller. There was no spare office within the area of the nose of the building, and so the swing doors enclosing this area were moved some feet so that his office came within the hallowed space. Very silly, as 'Benjie', as he was known, couldn't have cared less so long as he had a comfortable office close to all the other senior officers. In one of his gay moments, it was John Watt, the Head of Variety, who referred to this portion of the building as 'The Passing of the Third Floor Buck'. In his happy way he also referred to the entire building as 'It's No Use and the Seven Controllers'.

On the third floor as well there was a studio which was primarily for Religion – Services, Talks and programmes such as 'The Epilogue'. It was not consecrated because I understood if this had been done – it stood upon ground which would also have had to be consecrated – it meant that the Underground which ran under the building would suffer the same fate. The Underground itself was a nuisance because the studios, which had been built in the centre tower to protect them from outside noises, could not cut out the rumble of the Underground from time to time, about which nothing could be done, and all the studios and offices suffered from the trains.

There was a big orchestral studio on the first floor, used, apart from programmes, for general meetings of the staff which Sir John Reith would address. An organ was installed there which became a bit of a problem, for the noise from it penetrated through the building to other studios where productions were going on. The departure of Reith was a very sad moment to those who had served under him so long; despite his outspokenness and firmness he was immensely respected by everybody.

There was, and still is, one of the most important and certainly popular offices, that of the Duty Officer. Duty Office was and is where all distinguished speakers and others, and quite a number of staff themselves, used to call in; where if Duty Officer was in the mood you would get a drink from the hospitality cupboard. One of the Duty Officer's most difficult and responsible jobs was dealing with outside callers on the telephone, frequently in severely critical mood, and trying to calm them down and then later report, if necessary, to the producer or person at whom the criticism was directed. When the telephone rang, they didn't know what was going to be said to them. In particular, Duty Officer's problems arose during General Election time, when people with strong political views would not only express them but continue until it was necessary somehow to cut the conversation short. Furthermore, if during general election time the BBC had a short broadcast by the Communist Party, it was pretty certain that the telephone would get nearly red hot with the comments that were made.

When you went into the Duty Office, you never knew who you were going to see. It might be a leading politician, a man renowned in the City or big business, or it might be just another announcer, who had walked in for a chat. Reith was frequently there to order Duty Officer to make some report. Of course on all the great occasions, be they the death of a king or a Coronation, Duty Office had to take infinite care in dealing with callers, for in so many cases a caller would demand to speak to the Director-General or the Chief Engineer or some senior official, and he had to hive them off with great patience and considerable courtesy. All the ones that I have known had and have all the qualities required of them, and I think they enjoyed the job immensely providing they had a good assistant, which they always had.

Very distinguished people could sometimes be found in Duty Office – for instance, Churchill or the Duke of Kent. Especially during the War, after the air-raid sirens had gone, talk and gossip would flow freely, for they had to stay in the building until the 'All Clear' had sounded, and then they would be dispatched in an armoured vehicle to their destination.

Some of the phone-calls were very amusing. I remember listening on an extension telephone to a man who was really very angry indeed because the eleven o'clock time signal had been omitted (for a perfectly good reason), and he complained bitterly at the suppression of this signal, because he had got it all worked out in relation to his pigeons, and now there was no time signal he had to start training them all over again. He carried on on this theme for a quarter of an hour, which was quite pointless. Duty Officer could only be sympathetic and explain the reason for the suppression of the time signal.

Commissionaires from the entrance hall would come for help because they had found themselves incapable of dealing with some people who had called at Broadcasting House. I remember one man whom they could not get rid of because all he was doing was walking round and round the entrance hall singing at the top of his voice and demanding an audition. Duty Officer had to come out and gently persuade the individual to leave the building, which he did – still singing.

Now it seems that Broadcasting House is to be abandoned and a new home found for the staff and studios. The old Langham Hotel was one suggestion, but this was dropped in favour of the site of the old White City Greyhound Stadium close to Television Centre.

It is quite clear that 'BH' in its fifty-five years' existence did an immense job of work, especially in the War years. The new building at the White City will certainly be very well equipped with new and up-to-date technical facilities, which will be a joy to the Engineering Division, who have to work at the moment with equipment out-of-date and, by modern standards, clumsy.

JOHN SNAGGE

I boarded the King's ship. Now on the beak,
Now in the waist, the deck, in every cabin
I flamed amazement.

The Tempest

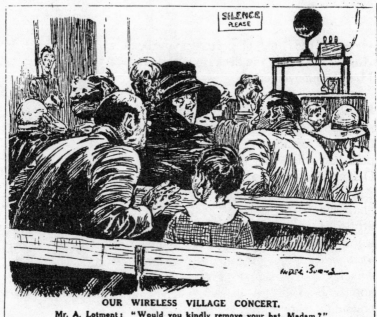

OUR WIRELESS VILLAGE CONCERT.

Mr. A. Lotment: "Would you kindly remove your hat, Madam?"

CHAPTER ONE

The Launching

BY 1932, THE DAYS of wireless concerts in the Village Hall had passed. Radio sets (annual licence fee ten shillings) had increased to such a proportion that 'Auntie' BBC was compelled to spread her wings. It was the year when Franklin Delano Roosevelt won the US Presidential Election and Aldous Huxley published *Brave New World*; when the Shakespeare Memorial Theatre first opened its doors at Stratford-on-Avon; the first Tarzan film was made in Hollywood; fans of Marlene Dietrich queued up to join her on the *Shanghai Express*; the Olympic Games were held in Los Angeles; and England's Harold Larwood became the least popular cricketer in Australia when he introduced 'body-line' bowling during the MCC tour.

No wonder 'Auntie' was getting restless.

Four years earlier, the rapidly expanding British Broadcasting Company had decided to build new premises in order to meet the growing public demand for programmes and to supply an adequate service. Sites under consideration had included areas in Aldwych, Kensington, the Strand and Portman Square; then one morning the BBC's Civil Engineer, Marmaduke Tudsbery Tudsbery spotted a FOR SALE notice outside Dorchester House, a Palladian-style building in Park Lane. He immediately set off to see the agents in Mount Street and asked to be shown over the property.

'Who do you represent?' the agents asked him. Tudsbery avoided a direct answer. He retorted: 'I presume it would not cost me more than half a million pounds?'

He was conducted through the large and elegant rooms and was impressed by the possibilities for conversion and expansion. He reported to his chiefs and strongly advised them that negotiations should be started for puchase of Dorchester

House provided the price was within the company's means. However, at this point Tusdbery chanced to be told by a friend that Foley House, a private dwelling with gardens at the corner of Portland Place and Langham Street was about to be demolished. Finally, this site, proving to have equally good opportunities as the Dorchester at far less cost, was cleared to make way for Broadcasting House. A formal agreement was signed with a Robert Bernard Solomon on 1 November 1928. (Mr Solomon was defined as 'the estate owner' in unencumbered fee simple in possession of the land formerly occupied by numbers 2, 4, 6 and 8, Portland Place and numbers 1, 3, 5 and 7 Langham Street in the Borough of St Marylebone in the County of London.)

The BBC's lease of the whole of the site and the premises to be built upon it was for a term of 99 years with the option to purchase at any time before expiration of five years from the completion date of the building. The rent was £45,000 per annum. The building was finished in 1931, purchased from Solomon for £650,000 and the freehold of the site was transferred to the BBC on 16 July 1936 with the proviso *inter alia* that:

> There shall not be used, exercised or carried on in or upon any part of the premises hereby transferred the trade business or calling of a Butcher Purveyor or Meat Slaughterman Fish Monger Tallow Chandler Melter or Tallow Soap Maker Tobacco Pipe Maker or Burner Smith Sugar Baker Fellmonger Dye Distiller Farrier Blacksmith Common Brewer Coppersmith Working Brazier Pewterer Tin Plate or Iron Plate Worker Tripe Seller Fried Fish Shop Coal Shed Keeper or Vendor of Coals Marine Store Dealer Rag or Fat Merchant Beater of Flax Autioneer Victualler Vintner Tavern Keeper Railway Parcel Booking Office Carrier Quasi-Medical or Quasi-Surgical Establishment Brothel or Bagnio Keeper.

A major difficulty that had to be overcome before building could commence was the presence of a deep sewer running diagonally across the site. Over 130 years old and brick-made, it was incapable of bearing any of the load of the 24,000-ton building. It had to be encased foot by foot in a reinforced concrete sheath before retaining walls and foundations could be constructed above it. The main function of this sewer, which was laid in chalk below strata of blue clay and sand, was to drain the surface water away from the Northern heights of London.

Tudsbery also had to steer clear of the Bakerloo tube railway, which still runs right under the centre of the road eighty feet below. In order to provide an independent water supply, an artesian well was sunk to a depth of more than 600 feet below sub-basement floor level at a cost of £700. This could yield if required one thousand gallons of water per hour.

On the west side of Langham Street, the Ellerman Estate insisted that there should be no reduction in light reaching their properties, and this resulted in the construction of the mansard roof on the east side of the building.

In accordance with tradition, various documents were buried under the foundation stone of Broadcasting House. These included copies of agreements in regard to the building and site, BBC documents of historical interest, the first copy of the *Radio Times* and other BBC publications and copies of the first three issues of the BBC *Year-Book*.

The Studio Tower, with its nine floors above and three below ground, forming the core of Broadcasting House, is entirely separated from natural lighting and ventilation, its twenty-two studios with waiting and listening rooms being lit and ventilated from a plant on the third floor below ground.

Ventilation and air-conditioning presented a major problem because of the required temperature conditions. The temperature in each studio, controlled and regulated by a thermostat, depended on the number of people using it at any one time. The air drawn in from outside passed through a chamber containing water sprays. On leaving the chamber, soot and other impurities were removed from the saturated air by a series of baffles before entering the supply duct. After cooling, the air was returned to the refrigerating plant in the sub-basement, the water coolers being situated on the roof. These are still there – they are independent of the wind, and the water temperatures can be accurately forecast under various weather conditions.

The sub-basement with its boilers, pumps and ventilating

plant with generators closely resembles the boiler-room in a
ship.

Initially, the two biggest studios were the Concert Hall on
the ground floor and that used by the military band on top of
the building. The BBC *Year-Book* for 1933 provided some
interesting statistics about the new land-ship, now firmly
anchored in Portland Place as a backcloth to the round Church
of All Souls with its tall, candle-snuffer spire tapering
heavenwards:

> There are 800 doors in Broadcasting House, the permanent
> crew approximating the same number – one door for every
> person. There is rather more than one radiator for every
> person (840 in all) whereas one clock to every eight persons is
> considered ample. Good sight is very important, so 6,500
> electric bulbs are provided – 8.125 to each occupant.

The golden lifts were then the fastest moving in London,
separate ones allocated to the crew and the performers.

The exterior of the new building was naturally compared by
some journalists of that era to 'a ship sailing down Regent
Street'. However, Mr W.K. Newson, MBE, the engineer
responsible for installing the equipment in the original Control
Room on the 'Upper Deck', said they were wrong: 'Broadcasting House is sailing *up* Regent Street', he stated, 'in the style
of the old iron-clad battleship. The bows face Regent's Park.'

The original building before the 'bows' were concealed by
the 1957 extension was judged by Professor C.H. Reilly of the
Architectural Department of Liverpool University, who wrote:
'One sees that the architect has taken the big curved front to
Portland Place and modelled it in a series of flat vertical planes
rising sheer from the pavement, but balanced about a central
axis, its overloading giving it the resemblance of a naval
aircraft carrier.'

When, on 18 March 1932, Stuart Hibberd made history by
reading the first news bulletin from Broadcasting House in a
small studio (4a), he was also well aware of the nautical
appearances. He observed that even the taps of the wash-basins
were of the press-knob type used on ships.

It was merely a coincidence that the BBC's Controller at that time was a Rear Admiral – Admiral Carpendale. His cabin was adjacent to that of the 'skipper', Sir John Reith. The circular rug on his floor was woven in the design of a compass rose, and woe betide anyone who did not replace it accurately after beating or cleaning!

For many, the most attractive adornments to the vessel were Eric Gill's sculpture groups. Shakespeare's Ariel gave him the inspiration for the 'airy spirit' listening to celestial music on the west front at first-floor level and below, poised between Wisdom and Gaiety.

On the east front, also at first-floor level, Ariel is seen piping to children.

One person who didn't appreciate Eric Gill's figures was the Unionist MP for St Pancras, South West, George Gibson Mitcheson, who then lived opposite the 'ship'. He particularly objected to Gill's creation of Prospero and Ariel perched on a globe of Portland stone directly above the main entrance, naked and unashamed. He was sufficiently disturbed to raise the matter in the House of Commons and to request that the Home Secretary should instruct the police to compel the BBC to remove the sculpture, which he said was objectionable to public morals. Sir John Gilmour, replying amid laughter, quoted the words of Mr Gladstone:

'I am not the official arbiter of taste or morals. I have no control over the decoration of private buildings unless they violate the law.' Capt. Cunningham-Reid intervened when the question was posed a second time with further laughter.
'Is it not a question of "Honi soi qui mal y pense?" '

The sculptor himself was most surprised by the number of complaints received from passers-by. 'It is beyond me altogether', he said. 'I am only a servant of the BBC, and if a statue is passed under the responsibility of Sir John Reith and other directors, it must be all right. Supposing I want to erect an immoral statue outside Broadcasting House. I could not do so. Ariel, the boy, is only ten years old. He cannot be offending women, and are men going to be offended? I think not.'

A more light-hearted view of Prospero and Ariel was taken by revue writers Eleanor and Herbert Farjeon, who, in a fit of midsummer madness, wrote 'A Masque of Broadcasting', which appeared in the *Radio Times* of 17 June 1932.

ARIEL: By what name, master, shall this house be called?
PROSPERO: Broadcasting House.
ARIEL: Where will you raise it?
PROSPERO: Where but in the heart of the most spacious City
   in the world!
ARIEL: How build it?
PROSPERO: As Amphion builded Thebes.
ARIEL: How's that?
PROSPERO: Hast thou forgot? That King of Old
      Seeing in his mind's eye the fairest pile
      The lordliest temples and the noblest towers
      Whereof man may be Sovereign, struck his lyre
      And built his walls to music. Thus will I.
             (*The music swells.*)
ARIEL: Lo, the foundation stone is laid on earth!
PROSPERO: Lo! the walls are mounting on the stories air!
ARIEL: A web of corridors! A tower of stairs!
PROSPERO: A myriad windows compassing the globe!
ARIEL: A hive for Gods to hum in. Lo, the roof!
PROSPERO: Broadcasting House is risen,
      More music, ho!

At nine o'clock on the morning of 2 May 1932, HMS Broadcasting House went into full service. In the role of the first Director-General, Sir John Reith hoisted the BBC's flag. Its special design, closely following the Corporation's coat of arms, consists of a terrestrial globe on an azure field, representing the earth with the seven planets in the sky around it. The eighth, Pluto, was not discovered until after the flag had been designed and registered.

The heraldic description of the coat of arms reads:

Azure, a Terrestrial Globe proper encircled by an Armulet Or and Seven Estoiles in Orle Argent, and, for the Crest on a wreath of the Colurs, a Lion passant Or, grasping in the dexter fore-paw a Thunderbolt proper. Supporters on either

side on Eagle Wings, addorsed proper collared 'Azure'
pendant therefrom a Bugle horned stringed Or.

The following morning, the 'skipper' addressed his mixed
crew of eight hundred in the Concert Hall and welcomed them
aboard. The sexes were segregated: men sat on one side of the
hall, women on the other. In a short speech, he greeted them
'not as staff in the mass but as individuals and hoped to get to
know each one of them personally'. He paid tribute to those
who designed, built and equipped the new headquarters.

Early visitors to the new building were particularly impressed by the bronze inscription in bold Roman lettering
adorning the wall above the main lifts in the entrance hall.
Translated from its Latin it reads:

TO ALMIGHTY GOD

The first Governors of this institution dedicated this Temple
of the Arts and Muses under the first directorship of John
Reith, Knight, praying for Divine help that a good sowing
may have a good harvest and that everything impure and
hostile to Peace may be banished from this building, and that
whatsoever things are sincere and beautiful and of good
report and lovable, the people, inclining its ear to these
things with a contentment of mind, may follow in the path of
virtue and wisdom.

On 14 May 1932, the last Savoy Hill programme was
broadcast and the Control Room there was closed for ever. It
ended with a mystery voice from the new building in Portland
Place announcing: 'This is Broadcasting House calling', to
mark the continuity of the service.

Two months earlier, on the night of 15 March 1932, the first
ever musical programme to be relayed from a studio in Broadcasting House was given by Henry Hall and his fourteen-strong
Dance Orchestra. His introduction to the programme was:

'Hello everyone, this *is* Henry Hall speaking', and his
signature tune 'It's Just the Time for Dancing' was composed
by Roger Eckersley, who was the Director of Entertainment
for the Corporation. He always played out with 'Here's to the
Next Time'.

Henry had been invited to lead a BBC Dance Orchestra in succession to Jack Payne, who left the BBC to tour the Music Halls. He had been recommended for the post by a Scotsman, William Mair, who was then Assistant to the first Head of Outside Broadcasts, Gerald Cock. Willie had heard, danced to and enjoyed the music played by Henry Hall and his band at the famous Gleneagles Hotel in Perthshire while on holiday the previous year. Henry Hall well remembers that deputation to Gleneagles with Gerald Cock, Roger Eckersley and Sir John Reith. 'You know, the first Director-General wasn't fond of music, especially dance music, and when my appointment was made, he raised his arms and wildly exclaimed "Halleluja! Halleluja!" '

Henry Hall's gentlemanly speech and appearance appealed to Gerald Cock, who knew he would not be tempted by the overtures of song-pluggers. Song-pluggers were rife in those days and wanted as many tunes as possible to be played in a single broadcast. Gerald detested snippets and found Henry to be a good ally in this respect.

Here is a glimpse of the ship's daily routine in those early days. At 6.00 a.m. precisely, the House Superintendent, Mr. Howard Chilman entered the reception area and addressed the Night Commissionaire: 'Time for the charwomen,' he said. The Commissionaire opened the doors to allow a steady procession of a hundred robust women cleaners to file through the hall. One by one they reported to the desk and saw their names ticked off in an enormous register. They themselves were ticked off if they were late! The Superintendent knew each one by name. 'Hullo, Mrs Jenkins, you're in number 15 to-day, aren't you? . . . Good morning Mrs Edwards, how's your daughter getting on? . . . Is your rheumatism better, Mrs Brown?' Off they all trooped to wash the decks and companionways, to clean the offices, armed with mops, pails and scrubbing brushes. There were 1,750 steps to be scrubbed and washed, for which in one year the BBC consumed 500 gallons of liquid soap. Every office inkwell had to be removed and cleaned everyday, while new ones were freshly filled to replace them. Following the cleaning squad's departure at 9.00 a.m., there came the advance guard of the 800 crew: girl typists and book-keepers, the telephone girls and the waitresses. The waitresses served 70,000 lunches a year in the shiny glass and aluminium canteen, where a satisfying meal then cost 1s 6d, with fish and meat dishes at 9d each, vegetables at 2d per portion and puddings and sweets at 3d. On the male side, engineers and studio attendants hurried in to prepare the twenty-two studios for the day's work.

In the front Entrance Hall, a man on a step-ladder arranged the lettering in a large metal frame giving the timetable of the day's output, including all the national and regional programmes and all rehearsals. In total the number of items averaged 250 hours on a single day.

Brightening each morning was the regular delivery of flowers, under the supervision of Eric Gill's sister, Lady Allen. In one of the long corridors (companionways), they were arranged in slim vases for distribution. In every studio and waiting-room these fresh blooms were displayed every morning. (They are sadly missed today.)

A TOUR OF BROADCASTING HOUSE

JACK DUNKLEY

Personally conducted by John Watt, tonight at 8.0.

Broadcasting House at work ..... Twenty-two studios in action ..... Vaudeville turns ..... The Wireless Military Band ..... Henry Hall ..... The Wireless Singers ..... The B.B.C. Theatre Orchestra ..... A Play in Rehearsal ..... Dr. Adrian Boult conducting the Orchestra ..... Television ..... Links with the Empire ..... The Chief Engineer in the Control Room ..... Christopher Stone ..... The News Bulletin in the Making ..... The Children's Hour ..... Talks .....

Tonight listeners will be able to hear what happens on the other side of the microphone in the new home of broadcasting,

BROADCASTING HOUSE IN ACTION

After the charladies had departed, the Reception Hall in Broadcasting House became a veritable bee-hive, with technical staff, neatly dressed secretaries and performers all converging. Producers, perhaps including Val Gielgud, would be hurrying from their offices greeting artistes, while the receptionists were summoning page-boys to escort others to various studios.

Henry Hall and his blue-coated musicians would already be on band call rehearsing new dance numbers in their basement studio.

Duty Announcers Stuart Hibberd and Frederick ('Freddy') Grisewood would be sitting in the News studio deciding who should read which bulletin and checking unusual pronunciations.

Children's Hour Producer, Derek McCulloch ('Uncle Mac'), might be discussing a relay from the London Zoo with the head of Outside Broadcasts, Gerald Cock.

As staff and performers dispersed, the white-coated Commissionaire might rush from the entrance doors to summon a lift. Into the Hall would stride the giant figure of the Director-General. There'd be tension in the ether as he entered the waiting lift to the salute of the Commissionaire.

The lift would ascend swifly to the third floor, where Sir John Reith took the helm for another day's broadcasting. His cabin in the 'stern' was furnished with oak-panelled walls, a private bathroom with coloured tiles, and a richly upholstered suite in pink satin, its flower-bedecked balcony overlooking the whole of Regent Street.

The day's programmes started at 10.15 a.m. with the 'Daily Service' relayed from the carefully planned studio 3E, designed by Edward Maufe, architect of Guildford Cathedral. Its chapel-like interior contained three tall arches and at the 'East End' was supported on four slender green columns with silver and gold capitals. The tall centre arched opening was shaped as a cyclorama and illuminated in such a way as to convey the impression of infinite distance across the silver altar. A vase of flowers stood in a white recess, upon which the shadow of a cross was reflected. The ceiling was delicately embossed with stars and crescent moons.

The very first morning service in Broadcasting House was

conducted in this studio by the Reverend Pat M'Cormick from
St Martin-in-the-Fields. He introduced the service with these
words:

> Our service this morning is being taken from the new
> Broadcasting House and I am sure you would like to join me
> in asking God to bless this place and this room, from which
> future services will be taken:
>> Here is a quiet room
>> Pause for a little space
>> And without faithless gloom
>> With joy upon thy face
>> Pray for God's grace.

Broadcasting House was also blessed:

> Oh God, whose never-failing providence ordereth all things
> in Heaven and Earth, bless Thee we beseech Thee all those,
> who have the responsibility of directing the affairs of this
> Corporation with courage and divine common sense, so that
> listeners may receive real recreation of mind and spirit; and
> truth may flourish and go forth unto the ends of the World.
> Inspire all who will speak, or sing or play, with noble ideals,
> that they may give of their best, whether grave or gay,
> instructive or humorous, and men may feel it is filling a real
> purpose in life for the common good.

During the peak hours of broadcasting, the Dramatic
Control Panel on the eighth floor picked up talk and music, as
well as noises from the Effects Studio below, and passed them
on to the Control Room itself, where all the studios and outside
lines were linked up with the transmitters. Next door in Studio
BA, the Wireless Military Band was broadcasting, while a
contributor waited to give a talk in Studio 3D, which had two
armchairs in front of an electric fire and a woollen rug on the
hearth. An adjacent Talks studio was furnished like a study
with walnut furniture and book-cases.

Throughout the day, men of varying trades manned the intri-
cate machinery by which Broadcasting House functioned, with
the support of engineering, maintenance and repair experts.

At 6.00 p.m., when 'Children's Hour' bid 'Good-Night', the Chief Announcer read the first news bulletin of the day, (known simply as 'First News'). Evening transmissions began and continued without a break until Close Down.

By midnight, performers, announcers and engineers had all departed leaving HMS Broadcasting House to the Night Watchman.

CHAPTER TWO

Full Steam Ahead

SINCE FOLEY HOUSE, THE building which used to occupy the site of the BBC's new headquarters, was the home of James Watt, inventor of the steam engine, it is fitting that sound broadcasting acquired the appellation of 'steam' radio.

It was originally intended that the Concert Hall should be a huge auditorium, in which symphony orchestra concerts with an audience should take place. However, some considerable miscalculations regarding space condensed the cubic capacity of Broadcasting House and the Hall was confined to the size of a studio.

Viola player and founder member in the BBC Symphony Orchestra, Norman Carrell, MBE, recollects the situation:

> One must assume that the architect, given the job of designing the stage, asked players how much room or space they took up when doing their jobs. If the players asked were oboe or clarinet, holding their instruments close to the body, the answer would most probably have been "about a square yard".
>
> 'Therefore the answer to the architect's problem was simple: 120 players × 1 square yard = 120 square yards, i.e. a stage measuring 6 × 20 or 8 × 15 or 10 × 12, the original width of the hall being forty-two feet.
>
> 'Unfortunately, these measurements did not allow for the tymps or percussion with all their equipment or trombone slides or the bulk of double basses, so that when the tymps, brass and quadruple wood-wind had taken their places on the new stage, there was no room for any string players, who numbered up to sixty!'

Rows of front seats had to be removed, and the strings were

seated off-stage until such time as an extension stage could be fitted. Consequently, as it was impossible to seat the entire symphony orchestra, they moved to Maida Vale, where the Corporation had purchased a disused ice-rink.

Nevertheless, the Hall was used as an alternative to St George's Hall for Variety shows. It was also regarded as being particularly suitable for the nightly broadcast of the religious 'Epilogue' and was regularly used in the 1950s for the long-running 'Grand Hotel' programme featuring the Palm Court Orchestra, who played against a background of potted palm trees.

June 1933 was regarded as an important month in the history of Broadcasting House and the Concert Hall for the installation of the new Compton organ, the first in the United Kingdom to be designed especially for microphone trans-mission, took place there. On its inauguration, a special programme entitled 'Opening the Organ' was broadcast to christen the instrument. Three notable organists were invited to perform: Sir George Thalben-Ball, Mr G.D. Cunningham and Sir Walter Alcock, supported by the BBC Orchestra (Section G) led by Manus O'Donnell, conducted by Adrian Boult. Following the Dedication and National Anthem, Sir Walter Alcock played a Choral Prelude by Bach followed by the same composer's Prelude and Fugue in D Major. Thalben-Ball followed with another Choral Prelude, 'Eventide', by Hubert Parry and a Fantasia and Fugue on the Choral by Liszt. Lastly, G.D. Cunningham rendered with the orchestra Handel's Concerto No. 4 in F Major.

The following year, reference was made to the organ by the Wireless Correspondent of the *Evening News*, who wrote:

That magnificent organ, which ever since its very expensive installation in the Concert Hall in Broadcasting House has been the plaything of the highbrow boys of the BBC, has at last been permitted to step down from its most severe dignity. Mr Berkeley Mason last night broadcast a short programme of light music on it. It was enjoyable. There is nothing unseemly in a fine Concert Organ playing good music of a simple, popular and joyful kind. It is to be hoped that last night's recital marks the beginning of a more human policy.

Organ music is not easy to broadcast. It is a job which puts the engineers on their mettle, but they certainly seem to have the Broadcasting House organ 'taped'.

There were occasions in those days when extraneous noises interfered with the transmission of programmes from the Concert Hall. A terse memo from a Programme Organizer to Studio Allocation on 16 February 1933 read: 'I understand that on Monday last the second half of the Chamber Music Concert in the Concert Hall was badly interfered with by Jack Payne's Band in Studio BA. We cannot expect people to pay high prices for seats at the Chamber Concerts, and when they get there, give them a mixture of chamber music and dance music.' The very first public performance in the Hall was given on 15 October 1932, when the following notice was widely displayed:

> The Public will be admitted to the Concert Studio on October 15th for the first of a series of seven Chamber Music Concerts.
> Tickets: (Price 7s. 6d., 6s., 5s., 4s., 3s., and 2s.) may be obtained from the Ticket Office at Broadcasting House and the usual agencies.

Lionel Salter, who was a Producer of music programmes and later became Assistant Controller of Music recalls:

> The Concert Hall had to be confined to the chorus (BBC Singers) small orchestras and recitals of all kinds. I remember giving live concerts there before the War with the old BBC Empire Orchestra. We used to start rehearsals at 11.30 p.m. and go on the air at 3.00 a.m., which did not please the singers.

Salter's main recollections of Broadcasting House centred on the studios and recording channels, which were constantly being updated. He remembers one studio manager whose habit was to put his feet up on the console and immerse himself in *The Times*, disdaining to notice what was going on in the studio:

> While presenting a series of record programmes, I kept by

me a mound of indiarubbers, which I would hurl at the window each time I wanted a disc put on.

At one stage I was music adviser to the Drama Department. One had to keep running up and down the narrowest of staircases to get from the Control Room to the studio. On one play, the producer had a large cast tearing round and round the place to get a certain effect she desired. In the course of this rampage, one of the extra-high screens protecting and cutting off the orchestra, which I was conducting, was knocked over, tossing my baton into the air. I fielded the screen just in time to prevent the violins being rendered unconscious. As we were hidden from sight, no one in the production realized why we had stopped playing and many minutes passed before we were rescued! I also remember during the opening week of the Third Programme, a soprano, who was fortunately not singing, for one movement fainted. I had to catch her while continuing somehow to keep the music playing during the 'live' broadcast.

Allied to the Drama Department, and a very important part of broadcasting, was the Effects Department, which Peter Duncan remembers joining on Christmas Eve, 1933: 'That was my very first look at Broadcasting House. Val Gielgud was producing a play and he'd invited me up to see if I'd like to have a job in the Effects Department. We were to meet in the Entrance Hall at 7.00 p.m.'

Peter nervously walked round Broadcasting House three times before he dared to enter. Timidly pushing open the heavy bronze doors, he walked straight into a big Commissionaire, who told him to report to the desk.

Down came Val Gielgud in an opera cloak with a little goatee beard, a very distinguished looking man with a sword-stick. He greeted me.

'Welcome to Broadcasting House!'

There was I looking for a job and I thought it was marvellous that this great man took the time to come down from the Control Room and let me watch his programme.

HMS Broadcasting House

HMS Broadcasting House under construction

Eric Gill's 'Prospero and Ariel'

From that day I became absolutely enmeshed in Effects. I loved this work, even though I had left Ecko Radio and it took me six years at the BBC to reach the salary I was getting there. Everyone who joined the Effects Department had to go through an initiation ceremony. You had to be dipped into the water tank. Brian Michie and George Inns did this to me, saying, 'You'd better take your suit off.' It was the only suit I possessed, and joining at £2 per week, I couldn't afford another one. I was plunged into the tank, where I made splashes for Val Gielgud's programme.

We had two Effects studios. One where you opened and shut doors and the main studio with more elaborate equipment. Very often we used to get young actors to come in for 'Children's Hour'. I remember Ralph Richardson and Laurence Olivier coming in and I used to make them help me do Effects. I would give them a whip to crack and ask them to open and close doors for me. Everybody mucked in then. No one worried about unions. Many years later, when I produced 'In Town Tonight' on television, I moved a chair a few inches and all the studio lights went out. I was forcibly told, 'that's not your job!'

Arthur Phillips joined the BBC aged fifteen as a page boy at Savoy Hill (£1 per week, plus 2s 6d dress allowance), and moved to Broadcasting House two years later and joined the Effects Department as an operator.

The Effects Studio in Savoy Hill was primitive in the extreme. It was great to get into BH with its double-deck studio, rather like an operating theatre in a hospital with this vast table with various patterns on, where you could produce different sound effects. There was a big bath. There were electric motors everywhere, a great thunder-sheet; in the corner, a big drum hanging from the wall, in which there was a pound of potatoes to make the sound of the Matterhorn falling apart. There was a large roller skate on a tin bath with rivets to make train noises, also a long bank of gramophone turn-tables on two decks. We thought it was absolutely marvellous. Here at last we had some wonderful equipment and knew we could make bigger and better effects. It was so satisfying to manufacture sounds out of the air. A Producer would say he wanted the sound of an avalanche and we would have to give it to him. Hence the big drum and the potatoes and so it went on, rather like that.

Another pioneer in the Drama Effects Department, David Godfrey, remembers a trick played on him by a colleague:

I was given the duty on a play being broadcast 'live' of making a shelf-clock strike seven. When the cue came for me to lift the mallet by hand, instead of getting a chiming sound, I got a dull, almost inaudible thump. The mallet had been bent away from the gong. On the following morning, I attempted to brazen it out with the boss.
  'Good morning, Charles!'
  The reply I got was:
  'It's not a good morning for you, my friend. What happened last night?'

Once, a breakdown caused the Effects Studio to go off the air a half-page before David received his cue for breaking a cucumber frame. He had to descend three floors to another studio, taking with him glass and heavy stone to do the effect at a microphone reserved for acting only, to the amazement of the cast assembled there.

One night, a play was due to begin with a portable gramophone (played by David) churning out the tune 'Deep Purple'. When he applied the pick-up to the disc, the record instantly rose in the air and rotated once with the turntable before falling off and being propelled into the corner of the studio!

One of the most interesting sections in the 'ship' has always been the Control Room, which initially was divided into two parts, the rehearsal and the transmission sections. In this room terminate circuits from all studios and all land lines from outside broadcast points, from other stations and from the transmitters themselves. It is the key centre of activity distributing different channels, originally just the National and the London Regional, day and night.

The study of studio acoustics has always been an important

part of BBC research work, an absolute necessity being the prevention of 'electrical' interference between the different groups of wiring in Broadcasting House. The total amount of wiring used within the broadcasting circuits would stretch for 142 miles. The complicated power wiring, signalling and telephone circuits had to be arranged in such a way as not to interfere with the equally complicated wiring carrying the actual music and speech intended for broadcasting by the transmitting stations. At that time, there was not an exact counterpart anywhere in the world of the Central Control Room at the top of Broadcasting House. Owing to its unique character, it was designed in detail by BBC engineers, working entirely on their own past experience and incorporating everything essential to meet the exacting requirements of programme producers: wireless check receivers, land-line testing equipment, amplifiers for relaying programmes to listening rooms, interval signal and Greenwich Time Signal apparatus.

Two floors, six and seven, in Broadcasting House were reserved for drama. That meant eight studios altogether and three dramatic control panels. The dramatic control panel, the nerve-centre of three or more studios, could be used for a single production to provide a vital part of the whole enterprise of radio drama. The wizardry of this mechanical facility much inspired Val Gielgud with its gleaming surface of battleship grey, its knobs and switches, winking red lights that glowed and vanished as studios faded in and out of operation at his convenience. Furthermore, its ingenuity provided him with the framework for his popular novel *Death in Broadcasting House*. His plot depended on the ability of the murderer to move around to different studios on different floor levels in split-second timing before strangling his victim during the performance of a play entitled *The Scarlet Highwayman*.

Eric Maschwitz, under the pseudonym of Holt Marvell, collaborated with Gielgud on the book, which they wrote during a sixteen-day holiday in the South of France, dictating the seventy thousand words to a BBC secretary. The Engineering Division lent them their blueprint of studio plans in order to ensure accuracy. One of the characters in their novel described Broadcasting House as 'a worthy edifice fitted to house the marvels it contains'. *Death in Broadcasting House* was later made into a film. Phoenix Films financed it to the tune of £18,000. It was made in only twenty-nine days for distribution by Equity British Films Limited and grossed £90,000 at the box office. The cast included Jack Hawkins, Ian Hunter, also Val Gielgud himself in his natural role of the play's Producer, with support from a galaxy of contemporary radio personalities.

In order that recordings of unlimited length could be made, the Blattnerphone, an invention of a German, Louis Blattner, was installed in Broadcasting House in 1932 with a second machine mounted alongside it on the seventh floor. The first person to have her voice recorded on the Blattnerphone in BH was aviator Amelia Earhart, who in another studio at the time was relating the experience of her solo flight across the Atlantic.

In September 1932, a third such machine was installed, increasing the playing time to thirty-two minutes to accommodate a half-hour programme. For nearly four years the Blattnerphone was the sole means of recording programmes. The Empire Service depended on it, and by 1934 it was possible to record, edit and transmit twenty programmes per week. These Blattnerphones were gradually taken out of service in 1935 when more sophisticated equipment was introduced by Marconi-Stille. The day of direct disc recording had arrived.

In 1933, Programme Head Cecil Graves approached Talks Producer Cecil Madden and asked him to start an Empire Department. Said Graves: 'I don't want you to tread the urbane path. You can do everything fresh, create your own ideas.'

'They were three merry years,' says Cecil, who produced every type of programme from music, Variety and drama to talks, outside broadcasts and all the other branches of entertainment that provide a complete broadcast service. He especially recalls an ambitious outside broadcast from Hampton Court: 'I used sixteen microphones, something unheard of in those days, plus a complete orchestra. There had been no music played there since the days of Henry VIII. The programme included works by Clifford Bax and William Shakespeare.'

A 1932 survey among overseas listeners revealed that the

most popular broadcast item of all from London was Big Ben.
One listener in Kenya was poetically inspired:

> Ah! Ben!
> To hear thee when
> The world's at rest
> Comforts my lonely breast.
> An African sun
> Beats on the path I run,
> But when my heart is sad
> Thy echoing voice can make it glad –
> For each deep note of thine
> Beats in my pulse, and stirs my blood like wine.

D.C. Green (Staff No. 1608), who joined the Engineering
Division in 1932, was involved in an unfortunate incident
concerning the famous clock:

On the seventh floor of Broadcasting House, we had an
enormous amplifier giving 1 to $1\frac{1}{2}$ kilowatts of output,
which was fed into four massive loudspeakers pointing down
Regent Street. Every day at one o'clock we used to relay the
chimes of Big Ben on these after testing the circuit for fifteen
minutes beforehand. There was an ON/OFF switch connecting the amplifier to the loudspeakers. One day I forgot
to switch this off, and started to test the circuit just as Big
Ben was sounding the quarter. I put Big Ben out at 12.45
instead of one o'clock, sending Regent Street out to lunch a
quarter of an hour early! The Engineer-in-Charge gave me a
right wigging.

'Variety' was the term used at Broadcasting House to
embrace vaudeville, musical comedy and revue, in fact light
musical entertainment of every kind. Most of these programmes
were staged in Studio BA, equipped with a stage, flood-lighting
and seating for an audience of sixty. However, because Variety
was then considered to be 'Auntie's' bread and butter, it
became necessary to expand to other studios. 8A was borrowed
from the military band, the Concert Hall was used, also
'number 10', an ex-warehouse by Waterloo Bridge.

One of the most popular Variety programmes of that era was John Watt's 'Songs from the Shows', for which Jack Payne's or Jack Hylton's bands and others played favourite songs, linked with informal announcements.

On 14 November 1932, John Watt directed a special one-hour programme for the Daventry National network entitled 'A Tour of Broadcasting House'.

Ron Genders, who joined the BBC as a page-boy at the age of fifteen, has a special memory of Gracie Fields, when she came to BH to take part in a Variety show:

I was called from the Reception Desk to take Gracie Fields to the Waiting Room before her appearance in the broadcast. There, artistes had to have their material timed and scores vetted by arrangers. There was the usual Announcer to introduce the programme; other artists chatting including Henry Hall, who was at the piano laughingly playing his very popular signature tune 'Here's to the Next Time'. When I told Gracie there was ten minutes to go, she stood up, told us all to sit down and gave a quick demonstration of how to dance 'The Black Bottom' and 'The Charleston', then the two most fashionable dance routines.

Everyone joined in the fun, when suddenly 'Our Gracie' said: 'Now let's all waltz to my new number. Henry, you don't need the music. You know the tune. Sing up everyone and away we go!' Gracie chose me as her partner, me a young nobody! I blushed. That song became one of her greatest 'hits'. It was called 'Because I Love You'. Even to-day, the next few lines that followed remain so true. 'I tried so hard but can't forget, because I love you'.

Someone came in to announce that the studio was ready. 'Ta, Ta, folks!' Gracie, relaxed as ever, disappeared to do her performance.

I walked down to the Main Hall feeling like a young Jack Buchanan or Fred Astaire, although I met them both much later in my travels. I'm sure Gracie never had a rival!

In 1934, Eric Maschwitz left the editorship of the *Radio Times* to take charge of the Variety Department, which included both the Variety and Theatre Orchestras. Soon they moved into the nearby St George's Hall, which together with the adjacent Queen's Hall was destroyed in Hitler's blitz.

Sir John Reith and the Programme Board eventually agreed to increase the amount of light entertainment to compete with Radio Luxembourg and Radio Normandie, who were capturing listeners from the BBC especially on Sundays, when the fare was mainly dull and heavy without any light music, in Eric's opinion 'as darkly entertaining as a damp Sabbath in a Lowland village!' This resulted in a complete division between Variety and drama, which allowed Val Gielgud to concentrate entirely on plays. A Danish lady, Marianne Helweg, combining beauty and brains, was play-taster in chief. She read four plays per day, one thousand a year as adviser to Val Gielgud. She could read in eight different languages including Greek and Russian.

Sharing popularity with Variety shows were the bands, who provided the late-night dance music from various hotels, restaurants and nightclubs in the West End at a cost of £40 to £50 per hour. Every night except Sunday there would be a different band broadcasting. It might be Roy Fox and his band from the Café Anglais, Lew Stone from the Monseigneur, Ambrose and his Orchestra from the Mayfair Hotel, Jack Jackson from the Dorchester, Sydney Lipton from Grosvenor House and a number of others to keep the feet of listeners and dancers tapping away until midnight.

Broadcasting House inspired several well-known composers. Following his popular *London Suite* containing 'The Knightsbridge March', Eric Coates gave us another suite, *London Again*. The first movement, 'Oxford Street' embraced the happy, bustling shopping crowds; the second, 'Langham Place', started with a roll of cymbals, then a gong before the three notes B-B-C were subtly played and the piece ended with midnight chimes.

George Posford, who had worked as arranger and accompanist at Savoy Hill, wrote a piece depicting the new Broadcasting House in music after seeing an etching of the half-completed building. It caught the spirit and atmosphere of the whole place.

Geraldo and his Orchestra rendered the first performance of Michael Carr's 'Regent Street Rhapsody' in a 'Romance in

Rhythm' broadcast. This composition told the story of a young playboy, who became suddenly aware of his wasteful style of living after leaving the artificial atmosphere of a nightclub at the top of Regent Street. From the deserted pavement, he saw the shimmering white façade of Broadcasting House in the early-morning haze. The dawn impression was exquisitely captured while the boy became acutely sensitive to the beauty and freshness of the outside world.

During Reith's captaincy, the 'ship' was 'dry', so that when a new Variety programme portraying life in a public house entitled 'At the Pig and Whistle' went on the air, listeners were much surprised.

Garry Allighan wrote in the *Radio Pictorial*: 'Yes, the BBC has a "pub". It is a studio, worse, it is on the same floor as the Religious Studio 3E, from which the Morning Service is given. It has an oak bench, pewter pots, mugs and men and women sit around, laughing, singing, jesting.'

'At the Pig and Whistle', pioneered by Charles Penrose, produced by Ernest Longstaffe, became a firm favourite with listeners, but in reality the pub was temperance. Nevertheless, as the interest spread, dozens of country pubs with wireless sets held their own 'Pig and Whistle' nights. 'Some of them challenged us to a game of darts,' said Longstaffe. 'They firmly believed our pub was a real one!'

Con Mahoney, who ended his BBC career as Head of Light Entertainment, Radio in 1978, was given his first job in Broadcasting House in February 1933 as a Liaison Officer in a small room on the first floor next to the General Office Pool, which housed forty girls, all highly competent short-hand typists.

My first impression was that I had joined a Call-girl Agency. The sort of call I used to get was: 'Hullo, this is Stuart Hibberd's office here. Would you send up Miss Brown?' Similar requests for young ladies to visit other departments were received throughout the day.

Two ladies I vividly remember were the elegant Mrs Christine Towler, who was appointed Night Hostess, and

Madame Dubarry, who ran the original restaurant in the basement of Broadcasting House. I was only receiving fifteen shillings per week, but I could have a three course lunch from Madame Dubarry's kitchen for sixpence including coffee. Also for one penny a day, one could have Indian or China tea with biscuits and on Fridays a portion of Fullers cake. In that restaurant there seemed to be the whole of the BBC in one grasp. Henry Hall and his Orchestra, the Announcers, everyone working on programmes. Always a lively scene.

We used to watch the Hunger-Marchers from the Northern mining areas pass BH. The BBC adopted the Gateshead contingent, for whom boots and shoes were collected for distribution by a Major Tate. In those days visitors were allowed in the building. It was the sole job of a Major Menzies to organise parties and escort them around.

During his time as Chief of Light Entertainment, Con Mahoney gave Terry Wogan his first BBC job as Presenter on 'Late Night Extra' following auditions to find new disc jockeys.

Probably the saddest night ever experienced in Broadcasting House was that of 20 January 1936, the night on which the BBC underwent the emotional task of reporting to the nation what it was told were the last hours of King George V. (It has now come to light that his death occurred some hours earlier than reported.) At 7.00 p.m., programmes including 'Music of the Movies' were running normally, but the King's strength was said to be ebbing and shortly afterwards Variety and dance music were abandoned. News Departments were anxiously watching the tape machines for the latest bulletin until, at 9.20, the News Editor of the Press Association personally telephoned the BBC's News Editor, Mr Coatman with the latest announcement: 'The King's life is moving peacefully to its close.' Silence descended upon Broadcasting House. The mood was tense. All working staff including commissionaires and page boys stood anxiously at their posts. By now all radio entertainment had stopped all over the country. Every fifteen minutes, Stuart Hibberd went into the News studio to repeat the above bulletin.

The news of the King's death was received by Coatman just after midnight. Visibly moved, Sir John Reith went to the microphone to tell listeners: 'It is with great sorrow that we make the following announcement: "His Majesty the King passed peacefully away a few minutes before twelve. The man we loved as King has passed from our midst. We voice the grief of the peoples of his Empire. We offer profound sympathy to Her Majesty the Queen and the Royal Family." '

Ten days later, a Memorial Service was dedicated to His Majesty. An internal memo from Chorus Master Leslie Woodgate to his singers stated: 'With reference to the Memorial Service in the Concert Hall, for which you are engaged, it is requested that all the women wear black and all the men wear black coats with suitable trousers. Men who do not possess black coats may wear dark suits but colours of any kind must be avoided. Black ties will be worn.'

The late monarch had fortunately lived to see the inauguration of a service that was close to his heart. By December 1932, the two sets of wireless masts in operation in Daventry had multiplied to the point where directional transmissions were being made on two wavelengths simultaneously with the provision of new stations. The Empire was at last linked together through what King George V had described in his first Christmas Day broadcast as 'One of the marvels of modern science.'

The King had continued: 'I am enabled this Christmas Day to speak to all my peoples throughout the Empire. I take it as a good omen that wireless should have reached its present perfection at a time when the Empire has been linked in closer union. For it offers us immense possibilities to make that union closer still.'

A special 1936 Christmas greetings-card with map bore the words:

The searchlights of broadcasting now play over the Empire for more than seventeen hours of each day and night. The New Year will be a milestone in the BBC's Empire Service. In the Spring, new transmitters and aerials at Daventry will be

bringing all Dominions and Colonies and many of the
King's subjects dwelling outside the Empire into closer
touch with Britain and with each other.

Broadcasts were relayed to the Australian Zone (9.30 to
11.30 a.m.); the Indian Zone (2.30 to 4.30 p.m.); the African
Zone (6.00 to 8.00 p.m.); the West African Zone (8.30 to 10.30
p.m.); and the Canadian Zone (1.00 to 3.00 a.m.).

While the programme to one zone was drawing to a close,
that for another zone was due to start, with the announcers in
Broadcasting House talking successively to each one.

Within the first few months of the service, 6,000 letters and
500 cables were received from listeners overseas. This response
steadily increased as the listening world was widened.

King George VI also spoke emotionally about the Empire
Service, when making his Coronation speech on 12 May 1937:

It is with a very full heart that I speak to you tonight. Never
before has a newly crowned King been able to talk to all his
Peoples in their own homes on the day of his Coronation.
Never has the ceremony itself had so wide a significance for
the Dominions are now free and equal partners with this
ancient Kingdom, and I felt this morning that the whole
Empire was in very truth gathered within the walls of
Westminster Abbey.

Following the King's accession, the menacing shadow of
Hitlerism continued to spread more widely across the
Continent until the fateful Munich crisis of 1938 served as a
dress rehearsal for the change to wartime arrangements, which
came into operation a year later. Preparations for war included
the rapid expansion of broadcasts in foreign languages. News
bulletins in French, German and Italian replaced normal
programmes for short periods each day on medium-wave
transmitters.

Meanwhile, demands grew for the BBC to provide more
light entertainment, and the number of Variety shows was
increased. 'Band Wagon', first broadcast on 5 January 1938
became a firm favourite. It produced a long, affectionate

partnership between Arthur Askey and Richard Murdoch. A scriptwriter invented the mythical flat, which they were supposed to share at the top of Broadcasting House as caretakers of the 'six time signal pips'. To the flat they brought Lewis the goat, Lucy and Basil, Cecil and Effie, the pigeons, Hector the camel (at present wintering in Egypt but expected home for Christmas) and their landlady Nausea 'Bagwash', a name that Murdoch spotted on the back of a laundry van while driving to the studio.

Halfway through the series, during one of their 'cod' school turns Arthur suddenly remarked: 'Keep cave, Stinker, Matron's coming!' There were protests from some shocked listeners, to whom Arthur responded: 'At my school, there was always someone called "Stinker".' The name stuck and Murdoch never lost the label.

2 April 1938 saw the retirement from HMS Broadcasting House of the first Controller, Vice-Admiral Sir Charles Carpendale, Sir John Reith's right-hand man and Deputy Director-General. A few months later, the 'Ship's' captain himself retired, to become Chairman of Imperial Airways. *The Times* commented on his departure: 'The BBC is not without its critics, and never should be; but Sir John can leave Broadcasting House with the knowledge that his pioneer work, now brought to maturity had not to wait for the approval of posterity . . . What the ether has lost, the air has gained!'

At Carpendale's departure, two naval buglers with five other naval ratings 'piped him over the side', special permission for the ceremony having been granted by Lord Chatfield, the First Sea Lord.

Admiral Sir Charles Carpendale had been much feared by newcomers to Broadcasting House, but Jean Melville, who was employed as resident piano accompanist on the 'ship', had a standing joke with him:

My working day might extend from anything like five or six hours to perhaps twelve or fourteen if we had a rush on and a late night show after a long day of auditions. I was always busy, the moments when I was sitting idle being all too few.

Whenever the 'Admiral' came into my studio, he would always catch me the very moment I was sitting at the piano doing nothing! It became such a coincidence that he always greeted me with a twinkle in his eye, saying: 'I see they are still working you very hard, Miss Melville!'

After working at Broadcasting House for a few years, Jean fell in love with a gentleman of the ballet, to whom she decided to get married. On principle, she thought she should let the BBC know, so made an appointment with Sir John Reith. The DG asked her if she desired a rise in pay. 'No, I want to get married,' said Jean. She tells the story:

Looking surprised, also relieved that I was not asking for a rise, Sir John said: 'I'm afraid that decision does not rest with me. The matter will have to be referred to the proper executives.' He pointed out the difficulties of having married women on the staff, then arranged for a conference to be held. My case was to go before a committee of seven, one of whom, Basil Nicolls (Controller of Administration) was away in the South of France. However, he returned a one-word cable: 'Yes'. The other officials weren't so prompt. My future husband and I were embarrassed by the delay. I had already called the banns and because of his work schedule, we eventually decided to get married on my July birthday at Marylebone Registry Office. The official permission from the BBC was granted after six weeks. We were on our honeymoon at the time!

Pianist Jean Melville had joined the BBC in 1927 after graduating from the Royal Academy of Music. Still active, well and living in West London, she was one of the earliest broadcasters from Marconi House. She then acted as pianist for Archie de Bear before becoming resident accompanist at Savoy Hill and later at Broadcasting House, which she always called the 'Big House'.

Jean had a special aptitude for accompanying in Vaudeville programmes and for putting nervous performers at their ease during auditions and rehearsals. Many times a grateful singer whose nerves had gone to pieces was saved from disaster by her cool, comforting manner. They would come up to her after the broadcast and offer her a tip of half-a-crown or five shillings, whereupon she had to explain that being a BBC staff member, she could not accept gratuities!

Jean remembers:

Not only beginners were nervous. Stage and screen Stars were often worse. That is where my second function of unofficial hostess came in useful. There was an official receptionist, Mrs Towler, known as the Night Hostess, who greeted the Stars on arrival, but it was when they entered the studio and saw the microphones that they went to pieces. Gloria Swanson was in a terrible state like many others. When Sir Harry Lauder first came to Broadcasting House, he wrapped the microphone in a bath towel!

I often left the studio at 2.00 a.m. after Empire Broadcasts and once played in a programme starting at 6.30 a.m. after working until 11.00 p.m. the night before.

My lasting impression of Broadcasting House was that it was a world of its own. I felt when I was inside it that it was the nerve centre of the larger world outside with vibrations reaching out to the farthest island.

Unhappily, vibrations of a different kind continued to echo across the frontiers of Europe.

CHAPTER THREE

Action Stations

ON 1 SEPTEMBER 1939 THE BBC was already on a war footing. On that day, the television service closed down for the duration, radio services for UK listeners being reduced to one: the 'Home Service'.

Following Prime Minister Neville Chamberlain's announcement in a broadcast at 11.00 a.m. on 3 September that Britain was at war with Germany, the single programme was being distributed from a wartime Control Room which had been set up in a small room in the sub-basement of Broadcasting House.

Peter Duncan was one of about twenty who were on duty in BH on what the comedian Robb Wilton (Mr Muddlecombe, JP) described for many years to come as 'The Day War Broke Out'. Peter said:

We all imagined that the bombing of London would start immediately. We all thought we were a prime target and likely to be killed. We had been instructed, when hearing the air raid sirens, to go at once to various dispersal points. My designated place was the Religious Studio 3E, where the Daily Morning Service came from.

The sirens sounded directly after the PM's broadcast. Obeying orders, I went to 3E, solemnly sat down in front of the altar and put on my gas-mask. After an interminable waiting period, I could hardly breathe. I removed the mask, sensed nothing was happening, wandered out into the corridor, where someone told me that the alert had only lasted five minutes, yet for over half an hour I had been sitting like an idiot all alone in that lovely old studio.

The Air Ministry had wanted to close down broadcasting

altogether in wartime because they said transmissions could aid enemy planes. Happily, flight trials resulted in the conclusion that reliable navigational assistance could be denied to aircraft attempting to take bearings on a synchronized group of transmitters until it flew within twenty-five miles of one of them, provided the transmitters were accurately powered and synchronized. The Home Office were keen for broadcasting to continue as a means of communicating with and reassuring the public and finally the Air Ministry's objections were overcome. The agreement reached with the Ministry was for the use of four high-powered transmitters to a group: Fighter Command was given the authorization to close down one or two transmitters in each group if enemy aircraft were plotted within twenty-five miles of them. If it became necessary to close down a third transmitter, then the whole group would shut down.

Cables ran from various studios to the Control Room. They passed through the control panel and were fed to other cables, which in turn passed them out to the transmitter. By the touch of a switch the emergency gear in the basement would come into action. This meant that the basement could function quite apart from the rest of the building, accommodating a thousand people. Steel, rubber-lined doors were fitted to all exits.

The shimmering façade of HMS Broadcasting House as seen by the playboy in Michael Carr's 'Regent Street Rhapsody' soon turned to a grey camouflage. The entrance was protected by a wall of sandbags and armed guards, while on the roof, the BBC's own air raid wardens looked out for enemy aircraft and falling bombs.

The liner had become a battleship.

On 18 June 1940, the day Italy declared war on France and Britain, General de Gaulle first addressed the captive people of France from a studio in Broadcasting House, telling them that the cause of France was not lost.

Leonard Miall, who was on duty in the European Talks Department received a call from the Ministry of Information requesting that arrangements be made by the BBC for de Gaulle to make his broadcast at 10.00 p.m.

Says Miall:

We did not then know that his speech had already been

approved by the War Cabinet and the Censor. After Director-General F.W. Ogilvie had heard the General's broadcast, he asked me to escort the General to his office.

Over a glass of sherry, the General surprisingly said – he had not yet been invited – that he was going to broadcast again at the same time tomorrow. At that time, it was difficult to make recordings at short notice because we only had six Recording Channels, which were in constant use for French, German and Italian programmes.

De Gaulle asked if his programme had been recorded. When I told him it hadn't, that it was not possible to record it at the last minute, he tore strips off me from his great height and accused me of not appreciating the historical significance of the occasion.

The Germans had entered Paris, and the evacuation of the British Expeditionary Force from Dunkirk had been completed. Winston Churchill urged the British people to brace themselves to their duties so that: 'if the British Empire and its Commonwealth last for a thousand years, men will say "This was their finest hour!" '

Only the most optimistic of our islanders, whether in or out of uniform, had the nerve to go on singing 'We'll Hang Out the Washing on the Siegfried Line'. Other popular songs of the year such as 'Over the Rainbow' and 'Sleepy Lagoon' were temporarily forgotten during that hideously unromantic period in our history when the enemy were a mere 23 nautical miles away from the White Cliffs of Dover.

The first Duty Officers in Broadcasting House worked overnights from 18.30 to 08.30 in close conjunction with the Controller. Peter Montgomery, the first full-time Duty Officer, was relieved in turn on the rota by Jim Thornton, Maurice Farqharson and Colonel Forty.

Montgomery recalls:

There was a skeleton Staff, most of the departments having already been evacuated to various parts of Britain. A large proportion of the Entertainment Staff had gone to Bristol. This was an unfortunate choice because the Germans started

to bomb that City before London. The Religious, Music and
'Children's Hour' personnel went to Bedford; Drama
Department to Evesham, Variety to Bangor, and so on.

The Administrative Departments settled down in large
country houses not too far from London. Consequently, the
only ones left in BH were those in Talks and News, who had
to remain at the centre of events to keep in touch with
Government and Service Headquarters.

One night, a mistake was made in a late News Bulletin.
Shortly afterwards the telephone rang in the Duty Room.
When I answered, I heard the familiar voice of the Prime
Minister saying: 'Get me the Senior Official, I must speak to
him!'

I hastily ran to the Concert Hall, where Staff were
sleeping, but could find no one who would answer to that
description. I returned to the telephone to tell the PM that, as
far as I knew, *I* was the Senior Official on duty.

Winston Churchill roared on with his complaint, but
before ringing off, courteously thanked me for listening to
him so patiently.

However, there were to be many more such calls and Peter
was the recipient of many of them. He remembers that
Churchill was always angry if he could not directly reach the
person to whom he wanted to speak.

He had a great habit of getting on the telephone himself to
the various Service Departments, partly perhaps to see that
everyone was properly engaged on his job and also perhaps
to show that he was on his own job himself, although it was
hardly necessary to prove it in that particular way.

He rang me up in the Duty Room on several more
occasions. On the first of these I had tried to tell him what he
wanted to know, when he broke in 'Sshpeak up! I can't 'ear
yer.' We became more accustomed to each other after that.

Sir William Haley (Director-General, 1944–51) corrobor-
ated: 'I remember being told that the Duty Room had started
to cope with Mr Churchill, who had a habit of ringing
Broadcasting House late at night or early in the morning.'

Before he was appointed War Correspondent, Godfrey Talbot was in 'News Talks', a little unit in Broadcasting House headed by Donald Boyd. This department organized such things as topical talks, especially after the 9.00 p.m. News. His job was to suggest, obtain and edit the contributions of speakers, also to look after VIPs when they came into BH to broadcast. One night Godfrey had to greet and bring to the microphone Lord Beaverbrook (the 'Beaver'), the powerful, hard-driving proprietor of the *Daily Express* who was also the dynamic Minister for Aircraft Production in Churchill's Government. He came to the studio wearing that 'hat'. He arrived, trailed by an obsequious PRO/speech-writer who was carrying his Master's papers, his own copy of the script and two bottles of the 'Beaver's' favourite Spa water, and a rubber cushion for his Boss to sit on during the broadcast. He was received in the Director-General's room, where he listened to the 9.00 p.m. News before being escorted to the basement studio. Godfrey recalled:

I was in the Studio whilst the great man performed. The servile PRO was ordered by his Master to crouch low on a chair facing him. Indeed he acted as audience and cheerer-on. He smiled, nodded, clapped hands silently, waved arms encouragingly; shook his fist whenever Hitler was mention-ed. It was a fantastic pantomime! I feared that he might overplay his role and actually raise a cheer!
Beaverbrook grimaced and growled through his speech, waving his arms to his servant, who was positively fawning.
Suddenly, without any warning, the studio lights went out. The 'Beaver' didn't panic. Evidently he remembered his lines and just growled on. I jumped to the wall near the door to bang my hand down on the point where I knew there were switches. One switch produced a dim emergency light to glow over the Master's script, which he soon completed.
We led the Great Man back upstairs to the waiting DG (Sir Cecil Graves) who, knowing about the light failure, was ready to apologize.
The 'Beaver' was not cross. He seemed delighted that he had triumphed over the blight of darkness. He said: 'I relish difficulties and fighting them. You succeed, or you don't.

I'm in a job where I might be the fall-guy, a job where I might get fired.'

Then, grinning like a gnome, he pointed a threatening finger at the DG. 'Like being Director of the BBC. *He* could be fired!' The Minister for Aircraft Production left Broadcasting House satisfied.

The number of aircraft in Herr Goering's mighty Luftwaffe was rapidly increasing, particularly bombers. London took the full explosive force of their attacks in 1940 and 1941.

A Programme Assistant who joined the Empire Service at the start of the blitz was a versatile young lady named Margaret Hubble:

We had a studio on the fourth floor of the tower. When the sirens went, which was pretty well every night, we gathered all our papers and schedule material and went down to the basement, where we had a small restaurant table, in what was known as the Restaurant Annexe. It was rather cramped to say the least. We had to stay in BH for three days and three nights non-stop. Then we had three days and three nights completely clear to get out of London, if that was possible.

Originally, anybody who stayed overnight was sleeping in the Concert Hall. Seats were removed and mattresses laid out. We found that system of sleeping was bad because we didn't get enough rest, so after a while we were allotted Studio L.I., which was still in use at night. It was all very difficult because very often there was no light. There were no batteries left for torches in those days, and if you struck a match, it smelled foul because the atmosphere wasn't very good anyway. You couldn't see where you were going, the mattresses being so close together, scattered around the studio, one under the grand piano. We used to put a plan up in the Office with the mattresses drawn on it. You had to put your name on the one you were going to occupy, but it wasn't always foolproof. One night I was the last one left working. I entered the 'dormitory' convinced I was under the grand piano. I groped my way along, feeling the edge of the mattresses, on which people were sleeping, plonked my hand hard on the one under the piano, where somebody sat bolt upright and said: 'Who's that? Is that you Hubble-bubble?' It was the Overseas Presentation officer, Duncan Carse.

I had to go out again, look at the plan to discover which mattress was unoccupied.

Shortly afterwards, Duncan was asked about our sleeping arrangements in BH by Matron, who was responsible for health. He took her in and showed her our studio camp. All the mattresses were piled up high. She was horrified to learn that first of all men and women had been sleeping there together. She was no less horrified when Duncan said to her: 'Well, Matron if you imagine that anybody has any energy left for anything other than going to sleep by the time we get to bed, you've got another think coming!'

Celebrity speakers used to come in for a series called 'Britain Speaks', which went out three times a week to North America. It was to tell the Americans what life was like over here during the war. I can remember J.B. Priestley talking about the lack of onions and how a listener had sent him an onion, and 'what a treasure it was'.

Among the other speakers who enchanted the girls was film star Leslie Howard.

Someone in the office had to take the speakers to a room either in the Langham opposite or in Broadcasting House to have a sleep before their broadcast began at 2.00 a.m. One of the girls took Leslie Howard along to his resting-place. He was a delight to everybody and said to his escort: 'Oh, please tuck me up!'

On the night of the bomb we evacuated down to the basement, which was full of people. Quite suddenly we could hear a whole stick of bombs falling nearby. Somebody rushed in to say that there was a great big hole in the side of the building. Idiots that we were, Bob Beatty, the actor, Arthur Phillips of Recorded Programmes and myself decided we would go up to investigate.

Walking up the stairs, we met a large policeman, who immediately sent us down again. At the time the bomb eventually exploded, we were not aware that two of our Staff had been involved in evacuating those working on the floors above. One of them was Duncan Carse, who was going

around the offices telling people to get out. He was standing
in the doorway of one of them when the explosion occurred.
The room quickly filled up with smoke and rubble but the
extra wide door-lintel directly above his head saved his life.

Another member of staff who had a narrow escape on that
night was a charming lady of Scottish ancestry, Barbara Booty
(née Thomson), who until recently worked as an Assistant in
the Purser's Office.

As the Secretary on duty from Talks Department, she was
busily typing the script for Lord Lloyd, who gave the ten-
minute 'Postcript' after the nine o'clock News read by Bruce
Belfrage.

During an air raid alert, the tower was supposed to be safe,
so anyone on duty at night had to use a tower studio as an
office. Fortunately, Barbara was ordered to descend to the
basement in the nick of time. The Studio (3E), in which she had
been typing was blown to pieces.

The Newsroom was right down in the basement. When the
bomb exploded, Bruce Belfrage, who was reading the Nine
o'clock News, heard a voice saying: 'It's all right, carry on!'
Bruce did just that, with pieces of plaster from the ceiling
showering down on to his script.

At about 8.35 that night, (15 October 1940), Duncan Carse
was approaching the third floor when someone running
downstairs shouted: 'There has been a hit on the building on
the fifth floor'.

Says Carse:

At that time there were one or two men on the stairs just
behind me, who heard that statement. We ran up to the fifth
floor together to find the electricians removing the fuses in
the West Corridor. We looked at the debris. There was not
much dust about, so one of us remarked: 'I don't think it's
gone off yet.'

We argued that it must have gone into the Music Library,
ran round to the North Entrance and looked in. There was
not much light and no sign of any damage, so we ran round
to the door by the lifts at the South End. There we were met

by L.F.B. Fireman G. Robbilliard coming out of the Music Library, who said: 'There's a bloody great bomb unexploded in there. I want volunteers for a working party to clear it.'

'The time was then almost exactly 8.40 p.m. I do not know what happened to the men who were with me, but I promised to join Robbilliard just as soon as I had got my programmes moved downstairs. As Overseas Presentation Assistant, I luckily knew what was happening and was free to cope with the situation because I was *not* actually on duty.

First I thought of Programme A coming from 4D, to which I went, only to find an empty studio. There was a thirty-minute recording (8.30 to 9 o'clock), and the announcer had gone downstairs.

I next ran down to the sub-basement to contact Control Room. I told them the bare facts, asking them how soon they could transfer Programme A to BB. Their answer was: 'In two minutes.' This was at $8.42\frac{1}{2}$.

I told Russell of European News at about 8.44 and asked him to clear BB. Then I found Gibson Parker in the restaurant annexe and asked *him* to get his French Staff down from 3E ('Ici la France', 8.30 to 9.00).

Again I went to the 4th floor and turned Chalmers and Miss Townsend out of 4C. On the way, I met Miss Allgood and sent her down. I was still worrying about the Programme Announcer, Brandon-Thomas. I rang up Overseas Presentation from Room 309 to ask them to find him if possible and to stop him coming upstairs for his announcement at 9.00.

Next I thought of the Monitoring Section in 3A, whom I told to move. They were reluctant to go, saying that they would have to stop work altogether if they did. We agreed that two male volunteers should stay behind if their work was sufficiently important to warrant taking risks. This was about 8.48.

I left the Monitoring Section to pack up their gear, then looked again into 4D for Brandon-Thomas. He was not there, but I found Prentice asleep in the gallery of 3E and got him on the move. The last of the French Staff were about to leave the studio. The time: almost exactly $8.50\frac{1}{2}$.

I ran down again but am not certain why. I think it was to look for Brandon-Thomas in BB. I went up again almost at once, met a policeman somewhere on the third or fourth floors, noticing that people were being shifted out of 3B, 3C and 3D. Time: 8.55.

I heard the lift going up to the fourth floor, guessed it was Brandon-Thomas going to 4D and caught him in the corridor. He picked up his programme material and went below. Time: 8.57.

Back on the third floor, I found Lord Lloyd, the Colonial Secretary, just leaving the DG's room and collected one of his dispatch cases for him. I then tackled the Defence man Gaetjens to get his official support to turn the Monitoring Section out of 3A at once. They were still dithering around, half-working and half-clearing out.

We entered the studio together at about 8.59 to give the Monitoring Section orders to quit.

I was standing two feet from the door into 34 proper, and four or five feet from the partition forming the north end of the DG's room.

The bomb then exploded.

When things quietened down, I shouted several times before receiving an answer from behind me. I reached back and found a girl – Miss Bennett.

The fumes were so bad that we could only see about six inches, but luckily the partitions of the DG's room had been blown down so that we were able to feel our way out. At about 9.05 we came out by the lifts and saw the DG. He sent Miss Bennett downstairs and I told him that there were people buried in 3A.

Here it is important to relate the experience of Divisional Officer A.F. Locke, who was summoned to the scene following a call to No. 2 Fire Station in Manchester Square. The report stated: 'At about 21.05 on the 15th instant, a call was received to a high explosive bomb and fire at the British Broadcasting Corporation, Portland Place.' A trailer pump attended and Mr Locke, who was at a fire in Bryanston Square, was informed. Mr Locke received the call by despatch rider and attended.

Locke:

I was informed of the call and upon my arrival found the fire had been extinguished. The crews were searching for the body of L.F.B. Fireman G. Robbilliard of the BBC, who was reported to have been on the floor prior to the explosion. He was found by the crews severely injured and badly burned, and was certified dead by a doctor who was in attendance. It was reported to me that two more persons were believed to be on the fifth floor and also several others were buried under the debris on the third floor and calling for help.

On the fifth floor, a rescue party had arrived and taken away two persons who had been injured in the collapse and thrown clear. Studio 3A, a room of about 24 × 12 feet, had collapsed under the weight of the floor above, and trapped in the debris were at least three persons alive. I asked the man in charge of the rescue party if he was ready to take over the searching of the other floors and he requested that the Brigade be allowed to rescue the persons who were trapped in the studio. I therefore called the crews down from the fifth floor and work of rescue commenced.

To release the first person, a woman, it was necessary to tunnel under the debris a distance of about eight feet, and as certain masonry and a ventilating shaft had to be jacked up, the breakdown lorry was requested.

The work of tunnelling was carried out by Mr Locke by means of a saw and his bare hands, and the woman, who was pinned in a doubled-up position between a door and some wooden partitioning, was extricated after two hours.

Mr Locke was awarded the George Medal for the skill and courage he displayed during the rescue operation.

Marmaduke Tudsbery Tudsbery had his own reminiscences of the enemy's attack on his battleship:

Ironically the exterior camouflage painting was completed on the day Broadcasting House was hit by a 500 lb delayed-action bomb. That night remained one of my most harrowing memories of the Second World War.

This bomb entered the building at seventh-floor level, and it came to rest on the floor of the Music Library on the fifth floor.

My Chief Assistant, H.M. Greathead, was on fire-watch duty that night. With a Staff fireman, he went up to the fifth floor to see whether they could drag the bomb to a spot outside the tower, where it could cause less of a disaster should it explode.

Greathead went off to get a length of rope, but had not gone many paces along the corridor before the bomb went off, instantly killing the Fireman (Robbilliard) and blasting Greathead right away to the end of the passage.

With his face streaming with blood, he accompanied me to the scene of the disaster.

The damage was very severe. Five of the floors within the tower were largely wrecked. The heavy transverse wall dividing the tower into two parts had an enormous hole in the centre. It was in imminent danger of collapse.

I had to arrange for a team of experienced builders to come early next morning to shore up the vast gaping hole in the Cross-wall with heavy timber until a steel frame could be erected to support the huge load of brickwork, which hung precariously above it and whose collapse would have wrecked the entire building. The danger of collapse was removed within two days.

Tudsbery had other interesting wartime memories. There was the occasion during the phoney war when the building of retaining walls for the extension to BH was being completed:

On May 20th, 1940, a horse-drawn lorry transporting material to the site fell into the open trench of the excavations. The time was 11.45 a.m. The lorry got caught up on the timber struts inside the excavation, and the horse fell to the bottom of the trench some forty-five feet below.

The recovery of the horse gave to onlookers in windows overlooking the site an exciting afternoon. (Alas! No TV service in operation then!)

Tudsbery also reveals:

One morning early in the war, I phoned MI5 to say that I thought it just possible that a Clerk of Works on my Staff was related to 'Lord Haw-Haw' ('Jairmany Calling'). I can't remember why I thought this might be so, for Joyce – the chap's name – was common enough in all conscience; there were three columns of them in the telephone directory.

However, I was told that my surmise was correct. He was the traitor's brother. He left the BBC, enlisted to become a Sergeant in the British Army. After the War, the renegade brother was charged with treason and executed.

Duncan Carse, who received official commendation following an enquiry for his efforts to save lives and help the rescue party, has remained critical of the procedure on that particular night. Had the offensive weapon been correctly reported by the Defence Officer as a bomb and *not* a detonator, he thinks all the victims could have been saved.

All BBC programmes were carried on without check that evening. Uncannily, at the same time as Bruce Belfrage was reading the nine o'clock News, the German News read by Carl Brinitzer went out completely uninterrupted from a nearby studio. Belfrage went on the air again at midnight, listeners still being unaware that anything unusual had happened.

An engineer, D.C. Green, recalls: 'The whole floor of the battery room was covered in a sea of acid. I helped Chief Engineer Noel Ashbridge carry up buckets of soda to nullify it.'

The 'chapel' in 3E (Peter Duncan's 'lovely old studio') had been wrecked, and manuscripts and letters were strewn all over the place. When the AFS salvage men rummaged through them, they came across a pile of Radio School Talks headed 'Early Stages in German'! They must have been blown across from another studio. It was also ironic that the only part of a certain manuscript found in the remains of the Music Library was entitled 'Our Changing World'.

Not long after that tempestuous night, a shower of incendiaries descended on the 'battleship' during an evening raid. A chief official, Mr B.E. Nicolls, suffered injuries caused by falling debris while he was working in his office. There were no staff killed on this occasion, but a twenty-three-year-old policeman, John Vaughan, on duty outside in Portland Place, was killed by the blast.

A third bad incident was the arrival of a land-mine in

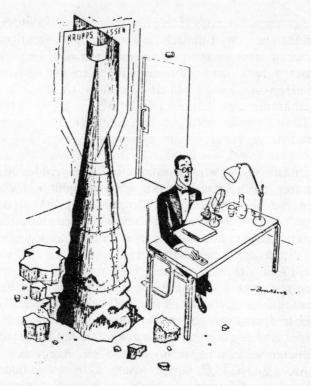

". . . and here is another bit of news which has just come through."

Portland Place near the front entrance of Broadcasting House. Luckily, there were few casualties, but there was much structural damage and part of the building was set alight, making evacuation compulsory. Duty Officer Peter Montgomery remembers leading a melancholy procession of staff to a rendezvous about five minutes' walk away, which had been rigged up in case of an emergency:

> We groped our way through rubble and broken glass, then, when I had delivered my charges safely, I returned to Broadcasting House to return various documents and see what had been happening. The ground floor was already waist-deep in water. Wearing only light shoes, I was deeply grateful to a stalwart fireman in waders, who picked me up and carried me through the flood.

One of the most prolific broadcasters then was the eminent novelist and playwright J.B. Priestley, whose programmes of encouragement and reassurance attracted a vast listening audience both in Britain and overseas. It was an extra broadcast to Canada, which he reluctantly undertook that saved his life in September 1940.

He had moved into the Langham Hotel to be close to Broadcasting House for his late-night engagements. He had done two broadcasts on the Sunday and would be working again late on Tuesday. Therefore, having a free night on Monday, he decided to return early for some much needed sleep. No sooner had he unpacked his suitcase than a message came from the Empire Service over the road begging him to do an extra broadcast on the London blitz to Canada. Growling and cursing, he agreed to do it and made his way to the studio.

After that broadcast, he didn't return to the Langham, because that was another night when bombs fell all around Broadcasting House. The Langham received a direct hit. The room in which Priestley had planned to enjoy a long night's rest was in the corner of the hotel that had been sliced off by a bomb.

George Beardmore, who joined the BBC in 1939 as Assistant Storekeeper, was roof-spotting on the top of Broadcasting House on the same night. To get there, he had to thread his way through streets barred to traffic and littered with debris. He remembered:

Some of the Langham Street windows of Broadcasting House were shattered and about a square half mile surrounding the building was roped off and evacuated. It looked even more like a fortress, splintered and scarred but not substantially damaged, unlike the Langham Hotel, which tumbled its top bedrooms into the street.

The following morning J.B. Priestley reported that he had seen parts of a London Transport bus perched on the roof of a building near Broadcasting House. They had been blown up there by the force of the explosion.

On the night that the 500-lb bomb had killed seven members of

staff, the office belonging to Cecil Madden and his Programme
Assistant, Jill Allgood, who saw the bomb lodged in the floor
of the Music Library, was completely destroyed. Jill suggested
to her boss that they might requisition a West End theatre (all
London theatres were closed at that time), preferably the
Criterion, which was underground, at least below street level.
She and Cecil 'squatted' there for a while believing the BBC
would have the powers of requisition, which they did.

The Criterion Theatre in Piccadilly became their HQ, but
Cecil also had at his disposal the Paris Cinema in Lower Regent
Street, which was taken over by the BBC as a wartime studio,
still used to-day, as well as the Prince of Wales and the
Queensbury All Services Club (now the Prince Edward
Theatre). 'My sleeping quarters at the Criterion were in a box
next to the Royal Box,' remembers Jill. 'Cecil's resting place,
little used, was in the Upper Circle.' Vera Lynn used to sing
there most evenings, and sometimes Edmundo Ros and his
band played all night.

Through his radio shows, Cecil Madden lifted many a
budding artist on to the ladder of fame. Petula Clark was only
nine when she was brought into the Criterion Theatre one
Saturday afternoon in October 1942 with a group of children
who were to send messages to the British Forces in Iraq. Names
had been canvassed overseas and Pet's uncle, a gunner, had
asked for her. The programme, 'It's All Yours' was directed by
Stephen Williams and produced by Cecil, who recalls:

> We used to give the children tea with buns, then Stephen
> taught them to sing the programme's signature tune
> 'Yours', made famous by Vera Lynn. We also asked if any
> child would like to perform, to sing another song or recite.
> No one ever did. However, on this particular day, a little girl
> courageously stepped out saying she would like to sing,
> adding 'with the Orchestra'. The orchestra were engaged in a
> card game. The conductor, Jack de Leon called them out:
> 'This young lady wants to sing with the Orchestra, boys,' he
> told them. 'We must not disappoint her, must we?'
>
> The card school players returned to their instruments
> unenthusiastically.
>
> 'What's your name, dear, and what are you going to sing?'

Pet's bold reply was: 'My name is Petula and I'd like to sing 'Mighty Like A Rose'.

She stepped on to the stage, extended her arms as she had seen crooners do and sang the song simply and with great purity. At the end the whole orchestra spontaneously applauded her.

Petula looked towards me. 'I can do some impressions, if you like,' she said.

'Who can you do?' I asked her.

'Oh, anyone. Vera Lynn, Sophie Tucker, Ann Shelton, Carmen Miranda, Schnozzle Durante.'

She cleverly impersonated them all. By that time, the programme was due to go on the air and she was allowed to sing in it.

Soon afterwards, Cecil let Petula Clark make her debut on the Home Service in an all-star broadcast with Arthur Askey, Richard Murdoch, Elsie and Doris Waters, Michael Redgrave, Geraldo and Vera Lynn on the vast stage of the Queensbury All Services Club.

Cecil has other wartime memories of the Criterion, where two of the front of house theatre staff, a Mrs Fenton, a cheery, caring 'Mrs Mopp' type, who wore an old-fashioned lace headpiece, and a Mr Brooks, who wore a bowler hat apparently permanently, had been retained. 'They were our caretakers and looked after us admirably,' he says.

In addition to his Light Entertainment operations, Cecil continued to do his work with his unit at Broadcasting House, where all through the blitz and beyond his Empire Service programme went out every day at 2.15 a.m. 'I used to walk up to BH from the West End on foot. If Chester Wilmot was back at base, he used to bring me a hot meal from the canteen.'

Mrs Fenton was worried that because of his abnormally long working hours with hardly any sleep, Cecil might develop stomach ulcers. Consequently she collected innumerable bottles of milk for him. 'This was much appreciated' says Cecil.

Sometimes she accumulated quite a big supply. One night following an air raid, the Tea Centre in Jermyn Street opposite the Criterion's stage door was ablaze. I joined a lone fireman with his hose. Between us we prevented the flames reaching the Criterion and extinguished the fire in the tea-house. The blast from that particular raid shattered Mrs Fenton's store-cupboard. The front entrance to the theatre was flooded with milk!

Protected only by her tin hat, Jill Allgood was frequently out in the blitz gathering programme material. Throughout the entire war, her programmes for the Pacific, African, North American and Home Forces programmes went out from Broadcasting House. She recalls:

My initial programme as solo Producer was a first broadcast to the West Indies. The star of that programme was that dynamic bandleader 'Snake-hips' Johnson. He was badly delayed by the blitz en route for Broadcasting House and I was desperate. He arrived in the studio only seconds before we were due on the air. That programme was very well received but sadly 'Snake-hips' was killed shortly afterwards, when a bomb went through the dance floor of the Café de Paris, the nightclub where he was playing. In the same club that night were the Nat Allen Quintet. They escaped injury but lost all their instruments. Fortunately Madden was able to find them replacements and book them for his next show.

The Talks Department always had a special relationship with the Duty Room in BH. Their speakers were chief guests and their producers regular visitors.

In his role as a wartime Duty Officer, Archie Gordon had abiding memories of their recollections and idiosyncrasies, particularly those of one, who later achieved a notorious place in our history, Mr Guy Burgess.

When Archie first met him in 1942, Burgess was Producer of 'The Week in Westminster', broadcast live on Saturday evenings. Later, Archie was to produce this programme himself, but unlike Guy Burgess he had not worked in the Foreign Office nor visited Russia.

In 1943, Burgess was proud of the fact that he had persuaded the BBC to put the first Communist MP into the programme.

Sir John Reith

The concert hall, June 1932

Gracie Fields in her final guest
appearance with Henry Hall, 1937

New equipment in the control room, 19

Leslie Howard and J.B. Priestley broadcasting on the Empire Service

The MP was Willie Gallaher, who had been recommended to G.R. Barnes, Director of Talks, as an outstanding 'Independent' who could be relied upon to play the game.

Guy Burgess had achieved his coup following a meeting with Sir Ian Fraser and Mr Harold Nicholson in Parliament concerning the matter of Independent speakers for 'The Week in Westminster'. This resulted in a decision by Barnes to allow an Independent to give one talk in twelve.

Willie was very nervous during his maiden broadcast but Guy kept him company in the studio for moral support. Said Archie many years later: 'I didn't realize at the time why Guy was so concerned for the success of that particular broadcast!'

As Producer of 'The Week in Westminster', Guy Burgess flattered MPs, who promised to help him promote his nefarious ideas, especially Labour MP Hector McNeil, whom he had known as a prewar journalist, and Tom Driberg, an influential columnist who held political views similar to his own. In 1956 Driberg obtained a scoop for his newspaper by exclusively interviewing Burgess and Maclean when they finally revealed that they had settled down to live in Moscow.

Director-General Sir William Haley was under constant pressure from Executives to promote Burgess to a more senior position in the BBC. Fortunately he withstood these pressures, because he took a strong dislike to the man. When Burgess departed to the Foreign Office he was extremely relieved.

That Burgess was not a likeable person was revealed in a report from the House Superintendent, with whom Burgess had a confrontation in Broadcasting House on the evening of 30 May 1941.

At approximately 7.50 p.m. on the night of May 29th, I was called to the Reception Desk to interview a gentleman who was complaining in a high-pitched voice of being unable to enter his room, No. 316, Langham Hotel. He complained that he had been waiting for an hour to get into his room, and carried on with a long story of complaint that the doors had no right to be locked – they were not allowed to be locked in other Government places and the whole system was wrong. Besides no one could enter to put out a fire, and he went on in this manner for several minutes.

I pointed out that I was unable to discuss the question; all I wanted to do was to help him to enter his room, and we were doing our best to obtain the master key of that room, to which he replied in a very loud voice: 'And a very bad best too!!'

He then asked who I was. Wasn't I a member of the Defence, and I told him 'No, I happen to be the House Superintendent at the moment.'

He then stated that the whole thing was most unsatisfactory, and continued to find fault with everything. Fortunately at that moment a Defence Patrol Officer came along. He told me he was endeavouring to obtain the master key, and would open the door as soon as he had contacted the Patrol, who held the key.

Mr Burgess then turned to the Patrol Officer and said: 'Well, go and get on with it!'

He spoke in such a domineering manner that the Patrol Officer took exception and passed the comment: 'You cannot talk to me like that. I am not a dog!'

He then proceeded towards the Langham Hotel followed by Mr Burgess.

I visited the Langham Hotel and found that the door of Room 316 had been damaged in an attempt to force it open by using a fire extinguisher, the contents of which were spread all over the carpet outside. I understand that the Defence Patrol is dealing with this matter.

The Defence Director took an even dimmer view of the behaviour shown by Burgess:

This report speaks for itself. Burgess behaved in a most objectionable and offensive manner. All this took place in the Entrance Hall in the hearing, not only of Commissionaires and other Junior Staff, but also of visitors, who were waiting at the Reception Desk.

I cannot have my staff spoken to in this manner and must ask for a written apology from Mr Burgess. The question of the damage he had done to the door and to the fire extinguisher, you will no doubt take up.

Guy Burgess did apologize following a reprimand, but said

that he considered that because the key took so long to locate, he was justified in using force to break into his office.

An interesting postscript to the brief career of Guy Burgess in the Talks Department appeared in the Letters to the Editor column in the *Western Morning News* on 14 February 1956. Mr R.S. Stafford of Yealmton wrote:

BURGESS WHEN AT BBC

Sir: I have just been reading the statement issued in Moscow by Burgess and Maclean. I was well acquainted with Burgess as I was Executive of the Talks Department of the BBC, in which he was employed before the War.

He states that he did not make any secret of the fact that he had been a Communist. This was not the case.

I knew that Burgess, though clever at his job of producing talks, was untruthful, idle and unreliable, but I never heard from him nor from any of his younger colleagues, to whom he talked a lot, that he had ever been a Communist.

It was my duty early in 1939 to inform him that in the event of War, he was not one of those whom the BBC would ask to be exempted from National Service.

Shortly afterwards he resigned from the BBC and joined a department of the Foreign Office. Later on in the War, he rejoined the BBC for a time, though not as a member of the Permanent Staff.

Burgess was interested in one thing only, that was himself. He was completely selfish and had no deep convictions of any kind.

I have little doubt that Soviet Russia will find him just as bad a bargain as did this country.

In BH the emergency Control Room (15 × 20 ft.) became extremely cramped and Studio BA was converted especially for its much-needed expansion.

It was then that 'Continuity' programming was first introduced into Broadcasting House studios. Each Continuity cubicle consisted of a control point and a place for the Announcer. At first there were only two cubicles, one for the Home Service, the other for the Forces programme. The system worked well then and still does to this day.

In 1942, Godfrey Talbot took over from Richard Dimbleby as BBC War Correspondent in the Middle East, occupying a makeshift studio in a squalid backstreet in Cairo, where the Arab porter kept his sheep on the ground floor. His recording room was sandwiched between a brothel on the floor above and an abortionist on the floor below.

While making his essential contacts at GHQ and the British Embassy, he had several meetings with the British Ambassador, Sir Miles Lampson, who was responsible for preventing King Farouk from following German propaganda, demanding and getting a more pro-British Egyptian Government appointed.

The Germans had been steadily advancing in the Western Desert and though temporarily entrenched behind the mine-strewn desert sands on the Alamein Line, they were reinforcing their strength for a further advance to capture the seaport of Alexandria. The lull gave the Eighth Army under the command of Lieutenant-General Bernard Montgomery the opportunity to gird their loins in preparation for the decisive battle that drove the Germans into full retreat and finally out of Africa.

With his colleague Denis Johnston, Godfrey Talbot was able to record for posterity 'Monty's' famous Alamein victory, giving on-the-spot descriptions of the fighting and explosive sounds of battle. Their M53 Recording Van was built by Army Workshops. It was their 'studio' and living-quarters combined.

All BBC wartime recordings were made on acetate disc. Tape recording had not yet arrived. In the African desert in Eighth Army days, the 600-lb weight of recording equipment was mounted in a 30-cwt Army truck. Some of the recordings were made in severe sandstorms.

The 40-lb 'midget' recorder was produced by the BBC Engineering Department. This unwieldy piece of equipment mounted on Army vehicles enabled War Correspondents to give actuality reports of such things as the bombers over Berlin and the airborne bridgehead at Arnhem.

The disc, often recorded under considerable difficulty, had to survive grievous hazards before it reached its ultimate destination. A record cut in the Western Desert – Godfrey Talbot in Libya for example – had somehow to be transported hundreds of miles back to Cairo. There it had to go through four different censors, Army, Navy, RAF and Egyptian Government. It then passed to a studio at Egyptian State Broadcasting for transmission to London by commercial beam radio.

Reception in London varied. At the final reception point in Broadcasting House, the Cairo transmission was re-recorded and at last the report was available for broadcasting.

Field Marshal Montgomery clearly understood the value of radio as an arm of warfare, firmly believing in the importance of morale in battle.

During that momentous year of 1942, William Beveridge started the Welfare State in Britain, Gilbert Murray founded Oxfam and G.M. Trevelyan wrote his *English Social History*. More important to broadcasting, magnetic tape was invented, and this was to revolutionize the technique of radio production in later years.

On the entertainment front, the lovely Greer Garson graced the silver screen as Mrs Miniver; Terence Rattigan achieved a notable success with his topical play *Flare Path*; the fabulous Bing Crosby set the box-office tills alight while 'Dreaming of a White Christmas' in *The Holiday Inn*, and Tommy Handley continued to captivate radio listeners with his scintillating comedy series 'ITMA' ('It's That Man Again').

'That Man' in 'It's That Man Again' was originally Hitler. The phrase was a *Daily Express* headline in 1938 and 1939. Every time Herr Hitler made one of his ranting, raving speeches, the front-page headline was 'IT'S THAT MAN AGAIN.' It appeared month after month. The journalist who coined it became Editor of the *Evening Standard*.

When Cecil Madden teamed Bing Crosby and Tommy Handley together for a 'Variety Bandbox' programme, Tommy presented Bing with an English pipe. This programme took place at Rainbow Corner, the American Forces Club in Piccadilly. Its leading lady was Kathleen Moody, now Lady Lew Grade.

It was from there that Madden compered the 'American Eagle in Britain' for five years. The programme was relayed in the States by Mutual and Don Lee in California. It had two helpers, Adele Astaire, then Lady Cavendish, who represented the American Red Cross, and Bebe Daniels, who contributed the Hospitals Spot called 'Purple Heart Corner' each week. Madden kept his promise to put on a show a day. Programmes were printed for each performance so that the American GIs could keep them as souvenirs or send them back to their folks at home.

A group of wealthy businessmen planned a meeting with Madden. Among them were Sir Simon Marks (Head of Marks and Spencer) and the Marquis of Queensberry. They told him: 'We've got a splendid theatre that you can use. What can you do for us?' 'We came to a gentleman's agreement,' recalls Cecil. 'They provided the lights, dressing rooms, all facilities including a manager. I provided all the shows. No money changed hands. It didn't cost the BBC a penny.' It was one of the happiest and most wonderful things to happen in wartime London. The theatre was at the Queensberry All Services Club.

At the Supreme Headquarters of the Allied Expeditionary Force, General Eisenhower was intent upon uniting the forces under his command, British, Canadian and American, providing a tripartite radio programme. Following delicate negotiations involving Eisenhower, Churchill and the BBC's Director-General (Sir William Haley), the joint AEF Programme was inaugurated. Maurice Gorham was head with the title of Major. Colonel Edward Kirby represented all the US Forces. No. 3, Cecil Madden, was in charge of all the integrated production. No. 4, David Niven, represented the interests of the Army Entertainments Unit.

Said Cecil:

The Americans asked for floor space in Broadcasting House and put their own guards in the foyer. With their large white helmets and boots, they were nicknamed 'Snowdrops'.

David Niven didn't like staying for meetings. He would arrive early before they started and say: 'I don't think I'll be able to help you this morning.' He would then disappear we knew not where but I had an idea he probably went to the secret Headquarters of SHAEF.

Those AEFP days were marvellous. With a flowing constellation of stars, I had such wonderful material. I could bring over artistes like Marlene Dietrich and Gertrude Lawrence on the same plane. I also had the services of top bandleaders: Glenn Miller, George Melachrino, Robert Farnon and Geraldo.

It was Colonel Kirby who was responsible for bringing over Glenn Miller and the whole of his Air Service Corps Band to London.

Glenn Miller had a big entourage. In addition to his sixty-five musicians were five vocalists, three Announcers plus several Arrangers and Producers. When they arrived, accommodation was a problem. Finally, the whole band were lodged in several different houses in Lower Sloane Street. That particular night was the worst so far for V1 flying bomb ('doodle-bugs') attacks. There were 'purple alerts' on the Battersea, Prince Albert and Chelsea Bridges. No sleep for anyone in that area.

Musicians don't like to be parted from their instruments, so the band stayed up all night guarding them. Next morning, their Organizer, Lieutenant Haynes, rang Glenn Miller.

'This can't continue,' he said.

Glenn rang Cecil. 'Can't we get them out of there?'

Arrangements were swiftly made to send the entire band to Bedford. Three large coaches transported them there, providentially just in time. The following night, the entire block they had been occupying in Lower Sloane Street was destroyed by a land-mine.

Miller's Company included men who were also bandleaders in their own right: there were drummer Ray McKinley, Mel Powell and Gerry Gray, as well as twenty string players from the leading American symphony orchestras.

Glenn appreciated the BBC practice of pre-recording. This enabled him to make personal appearances at USAF Air Bases at the same time as his scheduled radio programme went out on records. He was a strict disciplinarian, worked his men very hard and was always determined to get his own way of doing things. This latter trait resulted in tragedy. After the liberation of Paris, he was keen to go to Paris with his band. Maurice Gorham was doubtful if he could because lines from Paris were not sufficiently reliable to enable Glenn to maintain his schedule for the AEF. However, Glenn got over this hurdle by again pre-recording. He doubled his band's output to get a supply of eight weeks' programmes in advance.

Gorham was to write later:

> He and I had early clashes, chiefly I think because he arrived knowing nothing much about our set-up, thinking he was going to direct a programme instead of merely supplying a band... now, ironically enough, he was very grateful to me. As he was leaving my office in Broadcasting House after we had fixed it all up, I said to him: 'Now Glenn, there's only one more thing. For heaven's sake make sure the boat they put you on is seaworthy. We don't want to lose you all.'

On 14 December 1944, Cecil Madden heard a rumour via Bedford that Major Glenn Miller and Warrant Officer Paul Dudley were planning to fly to Paris in a private plane with Colonel Baessell of the USAF. He hurriedly took a taxi to the Mount Royal Hotel, where they were staying. He arrived to find them packing. Very firmly, Cecil told Glenn:

'Listen, I am your boss and I forbid you to go to Paris unless you go with your men. You must do that! You cannot do otherwise!'

Dudley agreed to conform with Cecil's request but tragically Glenn did not.

The band were due to fly in three Air Transport Command Dakotas from Bovingdon Aerodrome on 15 December but weather conditions prevented them. On 18 December, the three Dakotas were dispatched to Twinwoods Farm near Bedford. They took off from there and safely arrived in Paris with all their instruments. They never saw their leader again.

Major Glenn Miller successfully sought permission from the ailing General Goodrich, the commanding officer of the American 8th Air Force, to borrow his private plane, a UC 64A Norseman aircraft (U.S.A. No 44–70285). This ill-fated aircraft had only one engine, a one-way radio and no de-icing equipment. The lack of this facility was probably the cause of the plane's failure. Weather conditions were deplorable. The RAF told Morgan, the pilot, not to fly the plane but the USAF over-ruled them. The aircraft took off from Twinwoods Farm en route for Paris. The machine and its occupants were not seen again.

The RAF's Air Historical Branch considered the most likely cause of the plane's demise was that it was forced down in the English Channel by icing conditions, snow, sleet showers and bad visibility, which may have caused the aircraft to 'ice-up' and crash. They adamantly dismissed the theory that the aircraft was shot down. There was no German activity over the Channel that day. Indeed the nearest German fighter airfields were on the east side of the Rhine.

Cecil Madden has a strong feeling that owing to the lack of de-icing equipment and the atrocious conditions, the plane might not have gained height after take-off. He thinks it may have ploughed straight into the Chiltern Hills. Other dire thoughts that crossed Cecil's mind were that he believed the pilot, though considered competent, was not first class; that all the petrol was stored under the seats and Glenn was an inveterate smoker.

It was Christmas Eve before SHAEF officially announced Major Glenn Miller's disappearance. The bandleader was temporarily forgotten owing to the fierce 'Battle of the Bulge' fighting, in which the American Armies were being hurled back by the German Panzers on the Ardennes.

Six months earlier, in addition to the feverish planning for coverage of the Second Front invasion, Broadcasting House was mainly engaged with preparations for 'War Report'. The engineers provided a transmitter at Start Point, a network, and a wavelength on which to operate.

Archie Gordon, who was in charge of the Duty Room on D-Day, had become responsible for the maintenance of a confidential printed set of instructions called the Non-Engineering War Book, originally designed to chart the various operations to be carried out by the BBC in the event of invasion by the Germans or of the dislocation of central authority by bombing. There was now added to this small, black, loose-leaf binder, of which the Duty Room kept its numbered copy locked up, two new sections. One concerned the bringing up, on H-Hour Minus two, of an operational network of which non-engineers were told little. The other was the introduction of a new network of entertainment or information, jointly operated by the AEFP, SHAEF and the BBC, to be started on D-Day Plus One.

One was the Orange network, the other Purple.

On the previous day Archie Gordon was well rehearsed as to who would warn him, en clair, on an open line in advance of H-Hour and what he should then do:

I was chiefly concerned with the News Controller, A.P. Ryan, the Head of the News Announcer's Department, John Snagge, and the Senior duty engineer.

My D-Day log began:

05.55   'Warning from Hotline – something in the air – warn your Controllers'. I knew what this meant. It meant that he had received a message to bring up the Orange network, an operational service and part of the invasion communications system: nothing to do with the Purple network, the AEFP, due to come on air on D-Day plus One. I awoke only Ryan, sleeping behind a fusty curtain. His reply: 'Thank you. I'm waiting for the official message' and went immediately to sleep again. I admired his behaviour. I had lain on my truckle bed in shirt and trousers; he was in pyjamas. He was cool, whereas I was tremulous.

06.40   Ministry of Information called to summon Patrick Ryan and John Snagge to the London University Senate House, where the Ministry of Information had its headquarters.

06.56   Sir Ivone Kirkpatrick, Controller of European Services, and Ryan spoke on the telephone to agree on a common report in the domestic and European language bulletins reporting the Deutschlandsender news bulletin that Allied seaborne forces were approaching the Boulogne area. This was a faint movement, successfully designed to divert German attentions from the real beach-head.

None of the security arrangements could prevent its being broadcast and it caused fury to many official breasts. It was a good thing that Ryan stood firm and refused to instruct the Home News Editor not to put it out in the morning bulletins. At 7 o'clock, he and Snagge departed for the Ministry of Information where they were virtually locked in and put under guard by a combination of Ministry of Information and SHAEF officials pending the timing of Eisenhower's official announcement that the Allied invasion had begun. This was not broadcast until 09.32. Meanwhile, there had been one or two minor mishaps. The chain of messages to senior people in the BBC had not gone entirely as planned (through no fault of the Duty Officer) and the senior censor was also, naturally, in the Ministry performing that side of his dual role, when the American networks were screaming for his attention in Broadcasting House. I found his deputy in one of the two basement bathrooms splashing about and pushed him, still wet, to his office!

The News of the Allied landings in Normandy was broadcast in the Home, Overseas and Forces Programme. The communiqué was followed by a message from General Eisenhower read in the BBC Services by John Snagge and in the American Broadcasting Station in Europe by an American, Colonel Dupuy.

A congratulatory message on the faultless handling of the D-Day arrangements was received by the Engineering Division from the Chief of SHAEF.

At 0600 hours on D-Day Plus One, the signature tune 'Oranges and Lemons' heralded the start of the AEFP programmes broadcast by Start Point.

A week before D-Day, the first of the BBC's mobile transmitters with code name MCO ('Mike Charlie Oboe') was mounted in a 3-ton truck. This 250W transmitter had a rough trip across the Channel on 17 June in the tail-end of the gale that had raged in the Channel throughout the second week after D-Day. It arrived just in time; for the gale that had disrupted cross-Channel surface transport made it necessary for the Army type 399 transmitter, through which some of the early BBC dispatches had been sent, to be reserved exclusively for military traffic.

The operation was successful. The Broadcasting House transmitter flashed back: 'Reception quite satisfactory'. A link with Normandy was consolidated.

Discs from Midget Recorders were brought back by air or sea by Service Couriers to Broadcasting House, where Recording Channels were kept open day and night to receive them. These would often come from Correspondents, who had been ferried back to special transmission points in Britain, where they could send their reports 'up the line' to London. Correspondents and engineers having played their parts, the War Reporting Unit got to work to prepare the programmes for transmission.

'War Report' began its one-year history on D-Day. The programme continued until the end of hostilities with Germany. From the landings on the Normandy beach-heads to the final surrender of the Nazis, BBC War Correspondents gave on-the-spot commentaries on the fighting on the Western Front. Nightly, the reality of war was brought into the living rooms of millions of listeners, who heard graphic accounts of battle being waged from such as Frank Gillard, Richard Dimbleby, Chester Wilmot, Godfrey Talbot, Robert Reid, Wynford Vaughan-Thomas and others. They became household names. Their on-the-spot reports came from all theatres of war, some of the highlights being:

WYNFORD VAUGHAN-THOMAS describing a night raid on the Anzio beach-head:
The night sky illuminated by German flares . . . as bright as day . . . every tree, every house lit up. The flak from our own Ack-Ack Guns so heavy that our recording truck was rocking on its springs.

GODFREY TALBOT seeing exhausted Polish troops raising their flag over the ruined monastery at Monte Cassino:
The Poles had counter-attacked time after time. They hoisted the flag after a hard won triumph over an enemy, from whom they had suffered much. Men fought until they dropped exhausted, killed or wounded.

FRANK GILLARD watching trucks, jeeps, tanks, bulldozers,

ambulances, all kinds of vehicles being assembled:

In every wood and copse, in leafy dead-end lanes, embank-
ments, quarries, even private gardens, there were vast
numbers of these vehicles. I came across twenty-two men in
khaki shirts, battle-dress trousers and heavy hob-nailed
boots playing a game of knock-up cricket. They reminded
me of Francis Drake and Plymouth Hoe.

ROBERT REID surrounded by Parisians going 'mad with joy'
as they thronged down the boulevards into the heart of Paris,
again tasting the freedom of their own City.

It was one of the most dramatic scenes I have ever witnessed.
General de Gaulle was trying to control the crowds outside
Notre Dame . . . he marched straight into the Cathedral as a
hail of bullets were being fired by German snipers from the
galleries on the vaulted roof. Firing started all over the place
. . . I fell on the ground near the General. He marched
straight ahead without hesitating . . . his shoulders flung
back.

FRANK GILLARD announcing the joining of Russian and
American troops at Torgau on the Elbe:

East and West have met. This is the news for which the whole
Allied World has been waiting. Nazi Germany tottering to
her final collapse has been split clean in half. The forces of
liberation have joined hands.

RICHARD DIMBLEBY describing the horrors he came face to
face with in the 'liberated' concentration camp at Belsen:

Here, over an acre of ground lay dead and dying people . . .
you could not tell which was which. The living laid their
heads against the corpses. There was no privacy nor did men
and women ask for it. Women stood naked in the dust,
trying to wash themselves and catch the lice on their bodies.
Babies had been born there too weak and wizened to live . . .
This day at Belsen was the most horrible in my life.

ED BURROW counting out the paratroops as they jumped
into Holland:

There they go! . . . One, two, three, four, . . . seven, eight, nine, ten . . . fourteen, fifteen . . .

Every man out, every man clear. The whole sky is filled with parachutes . . . They are dropping just beside a windmill near a Church.

STANLEY MAXTED with the First Airborne Division seeing the supply planes coming in over Arnhem through heavy gunfire. The following year, he crossed the Rhine in a glider:

There was an explosion, which appeared to come from inside my head and a smell of burned cordite. I went down on one knee . . . There was a doom-like lurch. I saw my pal lying on one elbow with blood making a spider-web over his face. Bullets kept cracking through the wreckage . . .

Finally Chester Wilmot and Thomas Cadett, in at the end, reporting on the German surrender on a windswept hill, high up above the Elbe on wild Luneberg Heath.

During those six turbulent years of the Second World War, HMS Broadcasting House had surely endured her finest hours.

CHAPTER FOUR

The Lights Go Up Again

THE LIGHTS WENT UP again in London as Vera Lynn and Hubert Gregg had constantly reminded us they would. The flame of Lily Marlene was extinguished.

On VE-Day, HMS Broadcasting House was 'dressed over all'. Victory flags were hoisted on the stern. The Stars and Stripes, the Russian flag and the Union Jack fluttered in the breeze together, while the port side of the 'ship' was adorned with the flags of twenty-two Allied Nations. The whole was floodlit for the first time since the day of the Coronation eight years before.

The Allied Expeditionary Forces Programme in which American, British and Canadian men and women in uniform had worked side by side, came to an end. This enterprise had well achieved the aim of General Eisenhower, which was to cement relationships and morale between the three fighting nations.

Margaret Hubble, who made the closing-down announce-ment on the final programme, remembers that the AEF programme finished late one night in July 1945; that the same staff started the Light Programme the following morning with some extra Announcers, 'because we had all become British again'. She says:

> The office work was horrendous as we were coping with all the schedules for one programme, while dealing with totally new things for the next one all on the same day to get the show on the air in the morning. Maurice Gorham was still Head of this Enterprise. He took over straight away from doing his AEF Directorship to being Head of the Light Programme.

'Family Favourites', which started in August that year, had

the idea of providing a sort of Civilian Forces Favourites. We had to start it by inventing a programme because obviously we didn't announce ahead what we were going to do on the air. Several of us with friends and relations wrote to ask them what records they would like to hear and we used their names. I presented it and George Inns produced.

The result of asking listeners to write in with their own requests was sackloads of letters and postcards, which the Post Room were totally unable to handle. They had never received so much correspondence before. This mass ended up in our office at the back end of the fourth floor, which overlooked the empty pace at the fore end of Broadcasting House.

The Registry Department, when they were in evacuation in the countryside, had kept hens. When they returned to London, the hens came with them. They were being looked after down in this empty space.

George Inns came into the office one day in a frivolous mood, picked up a bundle of these letters making a jocular remark about the requests. He threw it across the room to one of the girls shouting, 'Catch, Rowena!' Rowena ducked in front of the open window and the package ended up right down in the gulf at the back there among the free-range hens, who started pecking at them. This incident resulted in a terse memo, addressed to me, because I was on duty that day, via our Programme Head with the remark that he didn't think the hens were on a sufficiently high grade to sort out the requests!

On 15 September 1945, an *Evening Chronicle* reporter wrote: 'The fortifications at London's Broadcasting House are being taken down by hand. Mostly they were constructed of solid cement, so their removal was no easy task.'

Speaking to one of the men engaged in the work outside Broadcasting House, he said: 'Looks like being a long job shifting those defences?' The workman replied: 'Looks like being a couple of years. When we opened up with the first pneumatic drill, there was such a to-do about the noise penetrating to the studios, where broadcasting was going on, that we had to drop it. Now we're back to the old hammer and chisel.'

Because the concrete blocks were six feet square, it was a formidable operation. It was over twelve months before the building started to resume its peacetime appearance, rid of its battleship-grey overcoat.

During the War, the Variety Department under John Watt's direction had fired many broadsides, achieving huge successes with shows such as 'Garrison Theatre', 'Bandwagon', 'Happidrome', 'Hi-gang', and above all 'ITMA', which was a firm favourite with King George VI.

The 'In Town Tonight' series continued to have an enormous following. In November 1957, Peter Duncan took over the production of that long-running, always exciting programme, which two years later celebrated its 500th performance. On that auspicious occasion, the team planned a surprise. Inside a large birthday cake, the engineers had contrived to sandwich a musical box. Composer Eric Coates was awarded the honour of cutting the gateau. As he did so, the knife made an electrical contact, which produced the opening bars of his 'The Knightsbridge March'.

Old stagers at the reception recalled that on the eve of the very first programme, the Producer, A.W. Hanson, realized that there was no signature tune. Gramophone Library were hastily alerted to send up to the studio all the records they had with London on their labels. 'The Knightsbridge March' from Eric Coates's *London Suite* was chosen.

'In Town Tonight' had been born in 1933, when Director of Variety, Eric Maschwitz, was looking for a new idea. Says Peter:

He approached the first ever disc jockey, Christopher Stone, who was much different to the present day disc jockeys inasmuch as he played some lovely music. Christopher suggested: 'Why not do a programme about interesting visitors to London?'

This was thought to be worth a trial. Eric thought it might go for six programmes. In reality it ran for twenty-six years.

In those halcyon days, Peter was free to travel to and from

America. Consequently he got to know the big stars in Hollywood. 'So many of them told me they would love to come on "In Town Tonight" when they came to London. They used to ring me up and say: "Hullo Peter, we're here. May we come on your programme?" It was like a snowball.'

Over the years, the glamour was provided by Judy Garland, Ava Gardner, Rosalind Russell, Greer Garson, Jane Wyman, Betty Hutton, Mitzi Gaynor, Mai Zetterling, Tallulah Bankhead, Gina Lollobrigida and hundreds of others.

For Peter, one of the most memorable programmes was the one in which Bing Crosby and Bob Hope sang 'We're off on the Road to Morocco'. What they really meant was that they were 'Off on the Burma Road', their own nickname for the formidable course at Wentworth in Surrey, where they frequently enjoyed playing golf together, when filming over here. It was the eve of a big Charity Match, which they were engaged to play with singer Donald Peers and comedian Ted Ray. All the lyrics of the Moroccan ditty were rewritten to become a skit on the golf match. It was the only time Crosby and Hope ever performed together in Broadcasting House.

However, as Terry Wogan soon discovered on his television chat show, you can't plan an interview programme on Show Business personalities alone. You must invite characters from other walks of life as well, ordinary people.

Anyone who has an interesting story to relate will always please both listener and viewer. One of the success secrets of 'In Town Tonight' was that there were no class distinctions. Dukes, dustmen, film stars, ordinary working people were bundled into the same programme and paid two guineas with expenses. Certainly, the appearance of Everyman and Everywoman made many people happier. Secretaries were busy after each programme forwarding letters from long-lost brothers, sisters and friends of those unexpectedly heard on the air. For a few, life was made easier. For example, a fire-eater was offered an engagement to tour Africa giving exhibitions of his skill, while a hawker who had rescued twenty-six children from the Regent's Park Canal was offered three jobs, one as Commissionaire, two as Caretaker.

Peter Duncan remembered that when he had big Stars on the programme, there would be as many as 300 autograph-hunters on the pavement outside Broadcasting House to welcome them, and that to coincide with the opening announcement: 'Once again, we halt London's traffic in order to introduce you to some of the interesting people who are In Town Tonight!' the police actually did stop the traffic.

They also controlled the assembled crowds. They were on extra pay and had a marvellous time. We invited them to the studio, where the atmosphere was always stimulating. Everything was 'live'. Because of that, you really did make friends. If you made an error, it went out 'live'. You relied on everybody. Everybody relied on you.

One evening I especially remember in Broadcasting House concerned that effervescent comedian Danny Kaye, who wanted me to instruct him about the English sense of humour.

We were rehearsing the programme and Danny, who was always fooling about, was getting a trifle restless awaiting his turn before the microphone. 'Come on, let's have a bit of fun with the engineers next door,' I said.

'What do I do?' asked Danny.

I said: 'It takes a long time to sort out all the cables because in the Control Room you've got to feed the National Programme, the Regional Programme and the Overseas Programmes. They are all going out through those wires. Just go along there and pretend you're going to pull them out!'

Danny marched into the Control Room, where the engineers were sitting, listening and manning the mass of complex cables as though they were doing their knitting. He grabbed hold of the 'knitting', wildly asking the engineers: 'What would happen if I pulled this lot out?'

They were terrified that he would really do so and put the whole Broadcasting Centre off the air!

Back from the war, which had made him a well-known broadcaster through his dispatches from the Front, Godfrey Talbot was made the BBC's Senior Reporter in the News Department.

I was not personally reporting. My job was really that of a

News Editor, marking the Events Diary, on what should be covered each day, marking which staff man we should send out to cover which job, although we had very few reporters at that time. As the first Reporting Organizer, I was given the task of recruiting and building up a Corps of specialist reporters; correspondents who would cover certain main fields of News. Then we scarcely had any such thing as a specialist Correspondent for any subject.

I began by getting the News Division to appoint a Political, a Parliamentary, a Science, an Education, an Air, an Agriculture and a Religious Affairs Correspondent.

Shortly afterwards, the Director of Talks, Sir Richard Maconachie decided that the BBC should have someone accredited to Buckingham Palace to do our own reports on what the Royal Family were doing.

Much to my surprise, because I hadn't thought about it for myself, I was told that my name was being put forward for the post of Court Correspondent.

After the Palace had approved the Post, I went to the Royal Household for a meeting with the King's Press Secretary, Commander Richard Colville, followed by a five minute interview with their Majesties. From then on, in addition to sound broadcasts at Home, I was to travel a quarter of a million miles commentating on Royal Tours.

When he joined the Control Room in Broadcasting House in 1946, Roy Maynard, like Danny Kaye, was amazed on first entering to see the huge mass of cabling in the sub-basement with the incoming bays and outgoing bays on one side and thirteen more bays on the other side. Bay One was the Green Continuity, in other words the Overseas Service at that time. Also in the Control Room area there were two Continuities – the Home and the Third Programme – whereas the Light Programme, the Purple Network, was up on the Basement floor. On a balcony surrounding the Control Room, there were remote facilities for transmitters along the South Coast.

Roy remembers working on a production of Brendan Behan's *The Hostage* with a brilliant Producer, John Gibson, who regrettably died very young:

I had set the studio up as a practical set, almost in the theatre sense. On one side of the studio, I set up a bed, a couple of screens. There was a bedroom, the living room and under the stairs, which were Effects stairs, we had the bathroom toilet. Also we set up the other side of the studio for a Scottish Ceilidh Band, which was an integral part of the play. One of the instruments was a bagpipe, a difficult instrument to balance under the best of circumstances. It was very difficult to fade it up in the studio, so we placed the bagpipe with the player right back in front of the lifts at the end of the corridor.

To be heard at their best, bagpipes have to approach the scene gradually from a distance. The piper started playing by the lifts, walking all the way along the corridor to the studio.

All the office workers on that floor were amazed at what was happening. They all came out to see what the noise was all about. The play worked very well, giving the Producer just the effect he required.

I was the Operator on the first six programmes in Studio B11. This was the first new Drama Studio purposely built for play production. We had had the use of Studios 6A and 8A in Broadcasting House and outside studios in the Piccadilly and Grafton Theatres. Now we were able to give these up. All our studios were contained in Broadcasting House.

B11 was large enough to produce Greek Tragedies. It was the first time we had a Control Desk with Quadrant faders. Up to that point we had always used Rotary faders. This was a great asset, a great step forward. Whereas before it needed two men to control tapes and grams, one man was now in charge of the overall mix. He could separate the tapes and grams on the panel itself and be in charge of the whole sound pattern.

In the winter following her Coronation, Her Majesty Queen Elizabeth II visited ten countries in the Commonwealth. Her broadcast on Christmas Day, 1953 was relayed from Auckland, New Zealand. A link-up with the Commonwealth preceded it. Called 'The Queen's Journey', this feature produced by Laurence Gilliam was broadcast from the Sydney Studios of

the Australian Broadcasting Commission in liaison with the
New Zealand Broadcasting Service.

These Royal Christmas Day broadcasts had continued
annually since 1932 but this was the first one to come from
outside Britain. It proved a technical challenge to the three
broadcasting organizations handling it. Of this occasion,
Maynard recalls:

In Britain the programme normally went out at 2 p.m. but
that year it went out at 7 a.m. The feed from Australia was
coming into Broadcasting House from five routes throughout the world. We recorded every route, so we had quite a
number of discs. (This was long before the day of recording
on tape.) Plans had gone ahead for a specially-beamed
programme at 11 a.m. that day, on what we were told was
going to be the best circuit. They had been on the air for
about ten minutes, when Geoffrey Bridson, who was looking
after affairs in the UK said: 'Listen, this is the worst circuit
we've had! Can you three Studio Managers get the best
quality recording on the air by 2 p.m.?'

The three of us sweated blood to get that programme on
the air in time. We just made it. Seven minutes into the
programme, we got a repeating groove on one of the discs.
Now, we remembered that on that disc, we had dubbed a
recording of the Queen's Speech sentence by sentence, word
by word, to get the absolute best quality. One of my
colleagues, Dennis Lewell, rushed it off to another studio to
see if it was all right. Luckily it was just as it came to the point
at 3 o'clock to play the Queen's Speech. It fell to me to play
it. I hadn't rehearsed it, so it was going over on two discs. In
those days, we used to do overlap or 'buck' changeovers
from disc to disc, each disc lasting about three minutes. I
wasn't sure which I was going to do. In the end I decided to
do a 'buck' changeover while using about an inch of
atmospherics we had on another disc to cover the join and I
got away with it.

There was a tragic end to this story. When the team
departed from Australia, Chester Wilmot, who gave us so
many historic on-the-spot war reports including that of the
German Unconditional Surrender, flew back by Comet, and

the plane vanished off the coast of Italy. His disappearance left a terrible mark on all of us. We had lost a dear colleague and friend on what would otherwise have been a happy occasion.

Brian Johnston, renowned for his lively cricket commentaries, joined the BBC in January 1946:

My first impressions of Broadcasting House weren't very good. I found the atmosphere claustrophobic, while the meetings I had to attend were boring. Senior staff had carpeted offices but there was no carpet in my office at 55 Portland Place, where several of us used to play indoor cricket to pass the time.

If an official telephoned from BH, we used to pull his leg saying: 'Would you mind hanging on until we finish the over?'

I remember working on an anniversary edition of 'In Town Tonight'. I did a cross-talk act with John Ellison. We wrote the script together. The next day we met Ted Ray, who complained that we had pinched all the jokes that he was going to tell in Henry Hall's 'Guest Night'.

In another programme on April 1st, Peter Sellers and I arranged to play a practical joke on Ellison. Peter came to Broadcasting House and we decided that he would impersonate my voice, which he did very well. On the night of the broadcast, he was on a microphone down at Oxford Circus pretending to be me, while I hid behind a screen in the studio. When I popped out towards the end of the programme, John Ellison looked as though he had seen a ghost!

I used to do a three-and-a-half to four-minute 'Live Spot' from different places of interest. Once I lay down on the railway line to give an impression of what it felt like to have the Golden Arrow speeding over me.

Even more scaring were the four and a half hours I spent one night in the Chamber of Horrors at Madame Tussauds. A national daily newspaper was offering a money prize to anyone who succeeded in spending a whole night alone in the Chamber. No one was able to do it.

I settled down among the murderers and villains, who gradually seemed to creep up on you. I felt like a jellyfish, cold and clammy.

After what seemed like an eternity, they reached the point in the programme at BH when Ellison said: 'Now, we'll go over to find out how Brian Johnston is!'

It was all very macabre. The sinister atmosphere gradually takes over and grips you. I was mightily relieved to get out of the Museum to return to the more congenial surroundings of Broadcasting House.

I stood in on several occasions for Jack de Manio as Presenter of the 'Today' programme, when he went on holiday. There were two editions. I was determined to avoid giving out the wrong time as he often did. I had a large card with the figure 7 printed on it for the first edition and another one with the figure 8 for the second.

Many years later, I walked into Broadcasting House one morning at the same time as Arthur Phillips, the Assistant Head of Outside Broadcasts.

'Have you heard the News?' he asked. "Jingle" is dead. We want you to take his place.'

'Jingle' was the nickname of Franklin Englemann. I followed him as the Presenter of 'Down Your Way' in October 1972.

Brian continued to present this broadcast until 1987.

In Variety circles, 1949 started on a sad note with the death in January of the comedian Tommy Handley, the idol of the listening millions. Twenty million heard his memorial Service broadcast from St Paul's Cathedral, while outside another two thousand listened through amplifiers and joined in hymns and prayers.

The choir, supplemented by the BBC Singers, sang Handel's 'Since by Man Came Death'. Then everyone joined in Tommy's favourite hymn: 'Praise My Soul, the King of Heaven'.

The Bishop of London, the Right Reverend J.W.C. Ward, paid his tribute: 'Who can tell how great a benefit he conferred upon our Nation in the days of its grimmest endeavour?' then spoke his epitaph:

> Teach us delight in simple things
> And mirth that hath no bitter stings.

On the evening of Tommy Handley's funeral, in place of what would have been the 312th issue of ITMA, the BBC transmitted a programme of 'Memories and Melodies' from the show, which had started in the summer of 1939. This memorial broadcast included excerpts from shows especially produced for Princess Elizabeth at Windsor Castle and for the Royal Navy at Scapa Flow. John Snagge read the linking narrative.

One of Tommy's favourite stories against himself was of the time when Broadcasting House called him to remind him that he was late for rehearsal; he was shaving, and he left in such a hurry he found himself out in the street, wearing pyjamas. Furthermore, he had left the keys of his house in his trouser pocket. As he scrambled to get back in through a window, it was only his famous password 'It's That Man Again' that saved him from being arrested by a copper passing on his beat!

By the autumn of 1955, the long-running serial portraying country folk, 'The Archers', had captured the attention of eight million listeners. On the night of 22 September they received a severe shock. For Archers fans, life would not be the same again after they had heard with sheer horror the last dying words of their beloved Grace: 'Phil . . . I love you Phil . . .'. Newly-wed Grace, played by Ysanne Churchman, died after being struck by a falling beam while trying to rescue a horse from a blazing stable at the riding-school.

For two hours, Broadcasting House was flooded with calls of anguish from sorrowing listeners. People were crying. Some drew their blinds, some cancelled evenings out, some collected wreaths, others asked where the funeral would be held and where flowers should be sent.

'Was it a coincidence that Grace Archer's violent death

occurred on the opening night of Independent Television?'
many were asking.

In reality, it was a closely guarded secret. Not even Grace's
father Mr Farebrother, played by Leslie Bowman, knew she
was destined to perish. The programme was usually recorded
in Birmingham, but that portentous week the whole cast had
been travelling down to London to record 'the secret episode'.

A resident in South East London wrote:

I thought I was in for a lively party, when I was invited next
door for the first night of ITV. Instead it was like a house in
mourning because Grace Archer had been 'killed off' in that
radio serial at 7.00 p.m.

How can people get in such a state over a harmless fairy
tale?

How can they get worked up over a bit of synthetic
sob-stuff?

Calls continued to keep the Broadcasting House switchboard buzzing for the next few days. A BBC spokesman said:
'She died in the normal course of duty. There has been much
regret, sorrow and some indignation.'

The Producer of the series said: 'I have no regrets about this.
Our aim is to make "The Archers" realistic. Tragic deaths do
occur in real life. If listeners are distressed by Grace's death,
that is all to the good because it shows that this radio family has
become real to them.'

The *Newcastle Journal* said in their leader (23 September):

Contemptuous laughter will ripple round the world at the
news that flowers were sent to the BBC from all over the
country for the funeral of Grace Archer. This will be
accepted as further evidence that the English are becoming a
nation of soft-hearted sentimentalists. Every person who
sent flowers intended for the funeral of Grace Archer was
perfectly well aware she was only a character in radio fiction.

On 26 September, the *Manchester Guardian* broke into verse
thus:

GRACE ARCHER

(Dulce et decorum est pro BBC mori)

She dwelt unseen amid the Light
Among the Archer clan,
And breathed her last the very night
That ITV began.

A maiden in a fantasy
All hidden from the eye.
A spoken word; the BBC
Decided she must die.

She was well loved and millions knew
That Grace had ceased to be;
Now she is in her grave but Oh
She scooped the ITV.

Finally the *Hanley Evening Sentinel* expressed their view:

As an example of showmanship by the BBC, I think it was a master-stroke. Its release on the night when the ITV network started was in our view a justifiable piece of counter publicity.

In 1959, the Newsroom was in Egton House, adjacent to Broadcasting House on the east side of Langham Street. Mike Broadbent spent two years there learning his trade before going up to Alexandra Palace and Television News, with whom he has been associated ever since:

The Egton Newsroom was full of characters who, as in so many walks of life, seem to be disappearing now. One of my earliest memories illustrates the agonies the BBC went through (especially in Engineering) over the fact that the ability to pull in actuality from around the world was a long way ahead of the quality of that actuality. It was used very rarely in News Bulletins in those days, being reserved for 'Radio Newsreel', which Cecil Madden had created in 1933 and was still going strong.

The argument between those who wanted to preserve the old values and us young, thrusting types, for whom News value sometimes outweighed quality, came to a head on April 12th, 1961, when Yuri Gagarin became the first man to enter space. The Editor of the day refused to use actuality of Gagarin's voice in the 1.00 p.m. News. It had appalling quality and was of course in Russian, that is when you could hear it at all. However, after a lot of heart-searching, it *was* used at 6.00 p.m. Something of a watershed!

During this period, I and a handful of colleagues were pioneering what were the Light Programme hourly summaries, now spattered all over the airwaves. There was no special studio, but they were read by the Duty Announcer in 'Light Continuity' in the basement of Broadcasting House. This meant that the Sub-Editor had to run down four flights of stairs from the Egton Newsroom into the basement, under the road along the tunnel connecting the two buildings, down another flight and along a corridor to the studio. As we were keen for the bulletin to be right up-to-date, we were always 'last minute', so arrived breathless. One morning I arrived to find an empty studio. Still panting, I read the News myself, the Duty Announcer having fallen asleep in the canteen!

On Saturday mornings, these summaries were read 'live' by Brian Matthew during his long-running 'Saturday Show'. As he presented this on the sixth floor of Broadcasting House, the Sub. tended to leave a little earlier. On one particular morning, my colleague Pat Chambers (with whom I still work in TV News) had left about 10.20, when we got a Reuter flash that Mr Khrushchev, during a speech in Moscow, had announced that the Russians had not only shot down the American U2 spy-plane but had captured its pilot, Gary Powers.

There wasn't time to think. I grabbed the Reuter tape, fled down the four floors, under the tunnel (because we were forbidden to use the lifts in case of breakdown) and ran up six or seven flights to the studio, being younger and fitter in those days. I reached the studio just as the last record was finishing, handed Brian the tape, told him to read it, while over his shoulder I subbed his original summary so that it still made the regulation one minute.

Out of the corner of my eye, I could see Pat's ashen white face appear round the edge of the window wondering where the hell this story, about which he knew nothing, had come from! Thanks to the professionalism of all concerned, not least Brian, we got a considerable scoop!

There was a long-standing Newsroom Duty Editor called John Beevers; a hard-smoking, hard-drinking, hard-swearing old hand, who quixotically wrote up the lives of the Saints in his spare time, being a fervent Roman Catholic. For this reason and because it suited his temperament to work virtually alone, he worked permanent nights, three on, three off, for as long as I knew him. All staff were subjected to Annual Reports, followed by interviews by Heads of Department. These were treated very seriously. The Head of our Division, Geoffrey Hollingworth, got more and more irritated with Beevers because he adamantly refused to come into the office during the day. Finally Hollingworth solved the problem by taking Beevers' Annual Report home with him one night, returning early next morning to arrest Beevers in Upper Regent Street. There, at his Green Line Bus Stop, the annual interview took place. A unique occasion.

Excavations for the extension to Broadcasting House had already started before the war, leaving a large hole at the end of the original building, which remained there for many years.

On 31 December 1955, it was officially announced that 'the BBC have let the vacant site adjoining Broadcasting House, Portland Place to the Prudential Assurance Company, who have agreed to re-construct an office building'. The Company were to lease the building to the BBC for a long term. The building was to be entirely occupied by the BBC, who would use it mainly for offices. Six five-storey-high Georgian houses behind Broadcasting House were pulled down to make way for the extension, though this progressive operation was held up for some time by an old lady, Mrs Jane Ellen Hawkins, who lived at No. 10, Portland Place, next door to Broadcasting House. She refused to move.

The construction of the extension finally commenced in

February 1957. The site, with an area of 250 feet by 200 feet, was bounded by Portland Place, Duchess Street, Hallam Street and Langham Street. The architects were Messrs Fitzroy Robinson and Hubert H. Bull with Sir Howard Robertson acting as Consulting Architect.

The design, especially the Portland Place elevation, won the approval of the Royal Fine Art Commission. Faced mainly in brick, with sliding sash aluminium windows, the main façade matched the traditional stone-faced character of Portland Place.

The extension was basically 'H' shape consisting of a central ten-storey pine block running East to West parallel to Duchess Street. At each end a seven-storey block faces Portland Place and Hallam Street. Adjoining Broadcasting House, the Portland Place wing was increased to a height of ten storeys to continue the general skyline of the existing building. The ground floor was designed to contain a garage for sixty BBC vans, mobile transmitters and Programme Control vehicles, and from the top of the building, the eighth-floor restaurant, looking north to the heights of Hampstead and south to the Surrey hills, offered attractive views.

In February 1965 the Board of Governors approved the proposal to take up the option to purchase the freehold of the extension from the Prudential at a cost of £1,850,000 (hitherto it was on a 99 year lease and the purchase would save £20–£40,000 annually in ground rent).

One problem in planning the new building was the ever-increasing volume of pop music. On the removal of the wartime Control Room from the sub-basement to the extension, the area vacated was once more used as a studio, from which to broadcast dance music. It was also intended for pop music, but owing to the high rate of decibels, it was found impossible to provide sufficient insulation for the Concert Hall itself.

An innovation with the BBC extension was a new type of studio for News and Current Affairs. New arrangements were made for all News dispatches from overseas to be recorded by Traffic Managers situated close to the News studio. This saved a considerable amount of time as Foreign Correspondents did not now have to wait for a Channel to become available.

Another important feature was the large modern Control Room, fully equipped with specialized switching systems and Control desks. This became the BBC's main London Control Room for the Home, Light and Third Programmes. Switching of programmes and associated circuits was made by remote control using motorized selector switches capable of switching any of 200 sources to any of 130 destinations. Included in the facilities is a TV Switching Centre responsible for the distribution of programmes to BBC Regional Centres and Transmitters. The building also houses a Central Communications Room, through which is exercised technical control over the whole communications network.

On the completion of the extension in 1961, Broadcasting House looked more than ever like a giant liner floating on that subterranean stream from Hampstead!

In the 1970s, Angela Bond, who started her broadcasting career as a pop music disc jockey in Hong Kong, produced the popular lunchtime entertainment programme 'Open House', which was presented by Pete Murray. Big stars of stage and screen used to appear. One of the most famous, Bette Davis, gave her first interview on radio in this country. The reason she had not given an interview previously was that, in America, reporters probe much more deeply into the private lives of show-business people. She didn't like that style of approach. 'I went down to Broadcasting House Reception,' said Angela. 'I stood waiting for this lady, whom I knew to be rather formidable.' She continued:

American stars usually brought 'heavies' or 'minders' with them. The doors swung open to admit a huge man, closely followed by a diminutive looking figure in a dark grey suit, a hat and long leather boots. She was tiny, like a sparrow as she walked in, but she gave me the impression that she was six feet tall. The presence she created was electric. She entered in a strutting manner like Queen Elizabeth the First. She didn't scare me but instinctively I knew that I would have to calm her down.

She was apprehensive. It showed in her slightly aggressive

demeanour. We addressed her as Miss Davis. I had time to think as we descended in the lift and walked along the carpeted studio corridor.

'What am I worrying about?' I thought. 'She's an American and all Americans love history.'

'Miss Davis,' I said, ' we are now walking through the part of Broadcasting House that actually housed the studios that relayed all those famous wartime broadcasts.' The actress was transformed. From being a high-ranking film star, she became an ordinary American grand dame. She raised her hands in the air, palms upwards, then pounded the walls, exclaiming: 'My God, you don't tell me. Wait till I get back home and tell them all about this!' From that moment on, we were on the same wavelength. She gave a lovely interview with Pete Murray, whom she described as 'a wonderful guy'.

Bringing many escorts was the heavyweight champion boxer Muhammad Ali, 'The Greatest'. He entered Broadcasting House with the biggest number of 'minders' I've ever seen.

There had been a buzz around the entire building that the famous pugilist was coming. He swept in behind his escorts carrying a large baby, a nine-month-old girl, beautiful but big.

Down we went but I couldn't get all the half-dozen escorts into the lift, so we decided to walk down the stairs, Muhammad Ali carrying his baby into the studio area. It was rather like a French wedding in the street, for I had picked up another twenty onlookers en route, all members of BBC staff. There was a huge retinue, a cross-section from almost every department. Even chefs appeared. The boxer looked fierce, but at the mention of the baby, he thawed. 'Her mam has gone shopping to Harrods, so I am taking care of her,' he said.

Into the cubicle, I managed to squeeze the 'heavies', agent and manager. By this time the corridor was packed with inquisitive people working in the building. I said: 'You may come in and see him, but only two by two for about thirty seconds otherwise we won't get the show on the air.'

Muhammad started a splendid interview holding the baby. Suddenly he pulled out of his pocket a feeding bottle and thrust it into the mouth of the baby, who appeared to be already overweight. The baby made sucking and gurgling noises, then, after finishing the contents of the bottle, emitted a loud burp of satisfaction.

The microphone was encased in a yellow windsock. The baby leant forward and gave it a playful left hook. (Her mother returned before the end of the broadcast to take over her child.)

CHAPTER FIVE

The 'Daily Service'

ASTERN FROM HMS BROADCASTING HOUSE is the rectangular Church of All Souls, one of the 'Waterloo' churches built as part of Britain's thanksgiving for the Duke of Wellington's victory over Napoleon.

In the early nineteenth century, more churches were needed to cater for the growing population of St Marylebone. All Souls was one of them. The chosen architect was John Nash, who was at work on his Regent Street plan at the time. When completed, it was consecrated by William Howley, Bishop of London on 25 November 1824.

The long and amicable relationship between Broadcasting House and All Souls started in July 1930, when Marmaduke Tudsbery Tudsbery wrote to the BBC's Director of Programmes as follows:

> This morning I had ocasion to meet the Reverend Arthur Buxton, Rector of All Souls Church, in connection with building operations in Broadcasting House.
>
> Mr Buxton would very much like you to consider broadcasting services from All Souls Church, especially in view of the fact that the Church is such a close neighbour to our new premises.

In his reply, the Director of Programmes said: 'When we actually move our office, we shall naturally explore the possibilities of the new locality.'

On 28 July the Reverend Arthur Buxton wrote to Tudsbery:

> I look forward to meeting you when you move into your new offices and I hope we at All Souls Church may have the privilege of broadcasting some of the Religious Services.

Early in 1932, engineering tests were successfully made on the organ and acoustics of the church, while permanent line installations were connected. A land-line forged a link with the Control Room in Broadcasting House for transmission over the ether.

The first broadcast of a Service from the church was on 19 June 1932 from 8.00 to 8.45 p.m. The Service included the hymns 'Light Abode', 'The Son of God Goes Forth to War', and 'Son of My Soul'. Also sung were the anthem 'Oh for a Closer Walk' and the Vesper 'Before the Ending of the Day'.

The address was given by the Reverend Arthur Buxton himself, who used to give a regular weekly broadcast from the Religious Studio, 3E in Broadcasting House.

A special Children's Service was broadcast on Sunday, 4 September 1933. Billing in the *Radio Times* stated:

This afternoon's Service has been specially arranged to welcome London Radio Circle Children to the Church of All Souls, Langham Place. Incidentally this is the first occasion upon which a special Service has been arranged in connection with the Children's Hour. The site is particularly appropriate in view of its proximity to Broadcasting House, the home of the Children's programme.

The Rector of All Souls very cordially invites all Radio Circle children, who may be interested to take part in this Broadcast Service, which will be heard by other children all over the country.

One thousand children attended that Service, but the Producer in charge was reprimanded for allowing the broadcast to over-run by seven and a half minutes.

Soon further Children's Services were relayed from All Souls, including one direct to the Empire.

On 26 May 1936, Director of Religious Broadcasting, F.A. Iremonger, wrote to the newly appointed Rector of All Souls, the Rev. Harold Earnshaw-Smith:

We have not yet had the pleasure of meeting, but I hope I may send a word of welcome to you, as Broadcasting House is in the Parish, of which you are shortly to take charge.

Please believe how much I hope that we shall meet shortly, and if you have time to come in for a talk and a cup of tea before you actually take over, I shall be very pleased to see you. There are many ways in which All Souls and the BBC can co-operate, and I hope that we shall have many opportunities of working together.

In the middle of the Second World War, All Souls was used as one of the commentary points for the programme 'The Home Guard in Action', which was broadcast on the Overseas Service on Sunday, 6 September 1942. In this programme a mock attack on Broadcasting House and its defence by the local Home Guard were described. It was a live broadcast enacted by BBC Home Guard members. Three commentators – Home Guards themselves – covered the exercise. With the Attack was Stewart MacPherson from Canada. With the Defence, Raymond Glendenning and Wynford Vaughan-Thomas. In Studio S2 in BH interpreting the action as it developed was Home Guard Michael Standing.

Introducing the programme, Standing narrated:

Point Zero – that's the wartime designation of one of London's most vital buildings in the very heart of the town – is about to be attacked. As I sit here in the well-lighted studio, I know that outside, through the deserted blacked-out streets, the enemy are taking up their positions. They are paratroops dropped at night by enemy transport planes.

Our information is that they have formed up, and in a few minutes they'll be ready to test the defences to the utmost. It sounds a desperate situation but we are not too worried about it, because – although there are real live Nazis less than 100 miles from where I am speaking to you in London – the paratroops are not Nazis, but Home Guards from a neighbouring unit, and the attack is a practice one designed to test the defences of Point Zero. All over Britain, men in the Home Guard take part regularly in exercises like the one we are broadcasting tonight . . .

The attack point given on the programme running order was listed as 'All Souls 2'.

Two years earlier, when a land-mine fell in Portland Place, All Souls suffered its first serious air-raid damage. The entire roof lifted, then dropped, bringing down the ceiling and breaking the main beams. The weight of plaster smashed most of the choir stalls and many pews; the spire was so severely shaken and twisted that the top thirty feet had to be pulled down. St Peter's Church in Vere Street was made available as an alternative place of worship.

The restored All Souls was formally re-opened after war-damage repairs on Sunday, 29 April 1951. It was then used continually for the 'Daily Service' from 1951 to 1975. Following the rebuilding in 1976, it has again been used as the normal base for a Service that originally started in January 1928.

It was to a listener, Miss Kathleen Cordeaux, inhabitant of a cottage in Bushey Road, Watford, that the idea of a broadcast daily service first came. Miss Cordeaux conducted a vigorous campaign. She was anxious for the preservation of a Christian Britain, also for the sick and housebound, whose spiritual needs she considered could best be provided by the wireless.

Displaying considerable energy, she gained widespread public support for her appeal for the daily religious service to become a reality. She eventually succeeded, thus helping to establish the longest-running radio programme in broadcasting history. The programme, which has changed very little in format since its inauguration, contains a bible reading, a prayer, two hymns and a psalm but no sermon. The hymns are sung by the BBC Singers (four men and four ladies) but the congregation are not permitted to accompany them.

The small congregation assembling at 10.45 a.m. each weekday in All Souls tends to increase in numbers during times of trouble, when churchgoers come to express their anxieties and fears. This was especially noticeable during the war in the Falkland/Malvinas Islands.

A Head of Religious Programmes, who shared in the broadcasting of the 'Daily Service' for sixteen years was the Reverend John Lang, who after leaving the BBC became Dean of Lichfield Cathedral. He has numerous memories of the Service, which he says was more enjoyable than anything else he had to do.

During the time I was head of Religious Broadcasting, I adopted a very conservative position about the form of the 'Daily Service'. Looking back over the years since I left, I do not regret that at all.

The 'Daily Service' provided the only genuine liturgy for broadcasting ever devised. It was brilliantly conceived by my predecessors. The books which they prepared for the use of listeners were admirable in every way. We kept them up to date without changing the essential quality of the broadcast.

We used All Souls as a very special kind of studio. Successive Rectors and their staffs were always helpful. We could not have done transmissions from a better place. Sometimes there were complaints regarding the noise of traffic outside, which we could easily have disposed with by moving to another studio. I considered that would have been a grave mistake. The roar of traffic was always an integral part of the worship which went on inside the Church.

One person I shall always associate with the broadcasts from All Souls was George Thalben-Ball. He was a delightful working companion, an outstanding Choir Master and Organist. I had the unenviable task of telling him that, at the age of seventy-two (twelve years after the BBC's retiring age), he would have to stand down. He told me he saw no reason for retirement, especially as he had just been re-appointed Organist to the City of Birmingham for a period which would take him well into his eighties!

One of the most important events in the history of the 'Daily Service' was the decision of the Roman Catholics to join us. It had always been a sorrow that only Anglican and Free Churchmen took the 'Daily Service', so that when Father Agnelus Andrew came to tell me that he and his Priest colleagues had been given permission to worship with us, it was a very special occasion indeed.

There was a real fellowship between the eight of us who were privileged to do these broadcasts. They were in fact the longest continuous series of any kind – longer even than 'The Week in Westminster'.

At the conclusion of one 'Daily Service' which he had been conducting, John Lang was assaulted by a burly member of the congregation, who punched him at the altar at the end of the Service, then speedily turned away and ran out of the church. John pursued his assailant down the whole length of Upper Regent Street. He overtook him at Oxford Circus, where the man struck him again. This time he was seen by a policeman, who quickly ran up.

The policeman asked the man what he thought he was doing. The attacker replied: 'Don't you know that I am Jesus Christ?'

'Well, it's your unlucky day' said the policeman. 'My name is Pontius Pilate.'

On another occasion, a female Spanish tourist came into the church in the middle of the Service. Not realizing that a Service was taking place, she demanded in a loud voice to be told the history of the building.

Veronica Lucas, a regular BBC Singer for 28 years recalls the morning when a charlady loudly interrupted the Service by calling out in a loud voice that she was looking for a job. The organist played louder and she retreated, but returned again after the psalm, shouting: 'Where's the caretaker? I want the caretaker!'

One day just as the Service was about to commence, a tramp arose from a bed of newspapers covering a rear pew, on which he had been slumbering. A commissionaire was summoned to deal with the dosser. As he dragged the protesting vagrant out of the church, muffled shouts and the banging of doors were heard on air as the incumbent was announcing: 'Welcome to the "Daily Service"!'

The Right Reverend Michael Baughen, Rector and highly respected Preacher in All Souls in the 1970s who left the Parish of St Marylebone to become the Bishop of Chester, was another who enjoyed the association with Broadcasting House:

We were particularly close together in consultation at the time of the rebuilding within All Souls in 1975 and 1976. There was a proposal for the Studio to be built at gallery level, but the sound insulation required alongside the organ was so considerable that the gallery would not bear the weight, and so the Studio Control Room was housed in the basement. Naturally the wiring up for microphones and direct contact to the Control Room and from the Control

Room to Broadcasting House was all within the planning of the new building. The chancel was intended to be carpeted but, at the BBC's request, it was eventually built in hardwood, to give a better reflective sound for the broadcasting of the 'Daily Service'.

A carpet was laid under the feet of the BBC Singers to deaden the sound of their feet on wood.

The BBC could not contribute financially to the rebuilding of All Souls but it was involved in personal interest from many broadcasters, not least from Terry Wogan interviewing some of the church volunteers, who were carrying out the old pews at the time the building project commenced.

Bomb scares were fairly familiar in London during that time. There had been an attempt to take through a plan for total rebuilding but this was opposed, causing considerable disappointment. Early in 1971, the Rector, the Reverend John Stott, expressed his frustration by saying that only a bomb could solve the problem. This remark received much publicity. The problem of providing a large hall for people to meet informally in the centre of London continued for several years. Therefore, it was not surprising that one evening when the doorbell of the Rectory rang at 10.30 p.m. and John Stott went down to open the door, his response to the policeman standing there saying to him: 'We have to tell you, Sir, that we have been told there is a bomb in your Church' was 'Praise the Lord!' Stott continues: 'The policeman was surprised at my spontaneous answer. However, we had to go down and search the church in any case rather than just hopefully leaving the situation!

'Subsequently, the plan for rebuilding within the framework of All Souls went ahead, worked out by Robert Potter, the architect. The magnificent achievement of his design is there for all to see.'

Kathleen Cordeaux would have been immensely gratified to read a certain letter received by Head of Religious Broadcasting, the Reverend David Winter, in July 1985 from a devoted listener in Thorpe Bay, Essex.

Dear Mr. Winter,

My widowed mother died earlier this month at the age of eighty-eight. I feel I must write to tell you what an enormous blessing the 'Daily Service' was to her during the later years of her life. While she was still active around the house she would arrange her 'coffee-break' to coincide with the Service. As she was unable to get out to her chapel during the last fourteen months of her life, the 'Daily Service' was one of her main sources of spiritual consolation and support. So often the Service, especially the Prayers, seemed to strike exactly the right note either for her own needs or for those of relatives and friends, in whom she was interested and for whom she herself prayed.

The late night (11.00 p.m.) slot was *too* late for her, but when the Evening Service was brought forward to 10.15 p.m., she was delighted and listened to every Service at that time until she died. She often spoke appreciatively of the evening services with a remark such as: 'What a lovely "cushion" to go to sleep on!'

CHAPTER SIX

The Purser's Office

SITUATED ON THE 'PROMENADE deck' behind the busy Reception Area are the offices occupied by the Duty Room Staff.

The post of Duty Officer is comparable to that of the Purser on board ship. His (or her) duties are manifold: provision of facilities for staff such as issuing traveller's cheques to reporters going abroad; urgent liaison with senior staff outside normal office hours, distributing information to the public, above all taking down criticisms from listeners to the eighty or more different radio programmes being broadcast every day. He or she also receives and entertains programme guests and VIPs.

At weekends and Bank Holidays, the 'Purser's' office is the main, often the sole point of contact for emergencies as well as routine matters. There is a constant demand from members of staff for the home telephone numbers of colleagues, whom they need to talk to urgently, usually with regard to programme production.

Many calls come from overseas correspondents and the BBC's office in New York. Consequently the Duty Officer and his Assistant spend a high percentage of their time on the telephone to the extent of approximately 60,000 calls per year. The ratio between complaints and appreciations regarding programmes is about 8 to 1.

Apart from the responsibilities outlined above, the Duty Office is always expected to be the fount of all knowledge. Sometimes it is regarded as being an information bureau:

'Can you tell me the height of the Eiffel Tower?' . . . 'Where are the next Olympic Games being held?' . . . 'My son is doing a school project. Can you tell him when Radio One started?' . . . 'My grand-daughter's little dog has run away. She is returning from holiday tomorrow. She will be heart-broken if he's not here to greet her. Please can you help me to find him?' . . . 'My husband is driving up the M1 to a business conference in Birmingham. He has left his briefcase with all his agenda at home. Can you relay a message to him? He always listens to Radio Two in his car' . . . 'The world is going to end in a few days' time. God is already here and he's taking over' . . . 'What was the lunchtime score in the Test Match? I missed it' . . . 'You didn't give the result of the Chelsea v. Tottenham game. Was it a late kick-off?' . . . 'Ray Moore says it's a terrible day . . . pouring with rain in Regent Street . . . tell him we're sunbathing in Manchester' . . . 'There is a strange orange-coloured object in the sky travelling westwards. It is very bright . . . maybe the Aurora Borealis . . . I thought you'd like to know!'

Sometimes it has been possible to cast a lifebelt to those in peril. On one grey November day in 1960, a life was saved after a woman listener telephoned in an extreme state of depression to report that her husband had eloped with another woman. She begged and implored that the BBC do everything within their power to seek out the philanderer and send him back home. In sympathetic tones, the Duty Officer explained that it was not immediately possible to meet her request. However, he managed to calm the unfortunate woman by telling her that he could probably assist her in another way. He telephoned the police to tell them of the woman's plight. They later returned his call to say that they had seen the abandoned wife, who had since been treated by a doctor, who administered sedatives.

The following morning, the police sergeant, who had acted upon the Duty Officer's call, confided that he very much doubted if the woman would have been alive today had they not arrived on the scene when they did.

On 24 July 1966, again with the co-operation of the police, the 'Purser's' Office was able to help with another delicate situation. This time the sexes were in reverse. A man who rang saying that he was sure he was about to go into a coma and, because he had an eighteen-month-old child at home with him, requested that an SOS message be broadcast to his wife asking her to return immediately. By its terms of reference, the BBC normally only broadcasts SOS messages to alert relatives urgently needed at the bedside of kin who are dangerously ill. Nevertheless, a 999 call from Broadcasting House to New Scotland Yard resulted in instant action being taken, which prevented any harm coming to the child. Two days later, the police called the Purser's Office to thank them for their assistance.

Many younger children may have been safeguarded by prompt action on a bleak midwinter's day in 1962, when a worried caller rang with an unusual but very human request. As snow and icicles were rapidly melting and falling from the nation's roof-tops, she asked if we could possibly warn mothers, who had left babies in prams outside tall buildings such as big department stores that their offspring could be in danger. The Duty Officer spoke to the Duty News Editor, who said he would arrange for this opportune warning to be broadcast. It was sincerely hoped that, in consequence, many babies would avoid an unwelcome bed-bath.

A large number of complaints telephoned to the Duty Office concern News and Current Affairs programmes, always vulnerable to public reaction. Frequently, accusations are made by listeners of left-wing or right-wing bias, sometimes the absence of a speaker belonging to a particular political persuasion. On this controversial subject, the Duty Officers are never permitted to take sides. They must at all times remain impartial when answering such calls. They have to suffer a small but regular posse of politically inspired callers, quick to seize any opportunity to take up cudgels in defence of the party of their choice. To these the Duty Officer and his Assistant lend an attentive, never a partisan ear. Some of these protesters are well-educated, others merely 'mixed-up'. The latter tend to get over-heated and muddled in their views, such as the lady who rang on 16 May 1975 after listening to a political interview on 'The World at One' to complain:

Where do you find all the gloomsters and Conservatives, who are always telling us what a state we're in? You only

have to see all the Rolls Royces driving around to know that
this is not so. Anyway, it is well-known that you BBC people
are all a bunch of bright Red Tories!

Another equally muddled woman once complained in
broken English that a certain Current Affairs programme had
given only one political viewpoint on a contemporary issue. 'I
am very much to the Right Wing,' she confessed. 'However on
occasions, I can conveniently turn to the Left! Good day!'
The Duty Officer was left fervently praying that he would
never have the misfortune to find himself driving directly
behind her on a motorway!
Some listeners think there is too much news, others consider
there is too much foreign news in relation to events at home,
while some would prefer to have no news at all. Ninety-four of
the latter group called in to the Duty Officer on 29 December
1975, the day on which a journalists' strike prevented any News
Bulletins being broadcast. One listener remarked: 'No news.
This is the nicest thing that has happened for a long time. Delighted to be without incessant news.' Others said how much they
had enjoyed a News-free afternoon. Many expressed their appreciation of the musical items that were substituted for the news.

'Congratulations on tonight's programmes. Much better to
have music instead of beastly news.'
'Delighted there was no 5 p.m. programme. So tired of
hearing continual news every hour on the hour.'
'Hope you lock the journalists out for at least a month.'
'I find it much easier to do the housework to music.'
'NUJ strike extension welcomed. A blessed relief not to
have so much news!'
'Very nice arrangement. You coped so well without it. So
much enjoyed not hearing any news.'

The final call was received from a lady in northwest London,
who said: 'If the BBC wants to save money, they have shown us
a heaven-sent way of doing just that to-day.'

Overseas visitors to the British Isles often comment that the inhabitants appear to care more for their pets than for their fellow human beings. Certainly, few natives would disagree that we are a nation of dog-lovers. One such addict telephoned the Duty Officer on a May morning in 1976 to try to persuade him that the BBC should broadcast an item with his thirty St Bernard canines on a magazine-type programme. He proceeded to request the room numbers in Broadcasting House of the producers he wished to call upon in order to sell his project. The Duty Officer explained to the caller that he should ask for this information on his arrival at Broadcasting House Reception Desk, but was much alarmed when the man also announced his intention to bring some of his 'best friends' with him. Very firmly, he informed him that it was strictly forbidden to bring dogs into BBC premises.

Temporarily losing his scent, the Master of the thirty hounds made a counter-attack the following day with kennel-hands and his entire pack when attempting to invade another BBC building, the Aeolian Hall in Bond Street. His attack was repelled by the BBC's Central Services Department, who were obliged to summon the police to deal with the sudden invasion.

Nineteen years earlier, on 9 December 1951, Lord and Lady Radcliffe, accompanied by a lone terrier named 'Rusty', were halted by the Commissionaire on their arrival in the vestibule at Broadcasting House. The Duty Officer in charge that day logged:

Lord Radcliffe knows our rule very well, but his Lordship nonchalantly stated: 'No dog, no broadcast.' – A Lord of Appeal in Ordinary can be rather difficult.

Back in the days of the Home Service and Light Programmes, when a man telephoned to ask if it were possible that he heard a dog barking on Radio Newsreel, the Duty Officer assured him that there had not been a dog in the studio.

The man was frustrated, saying that he had come up to London for the day with his dog, which he had lost in the vicinity of Broadcasting House. He thought that the 'little fellow' might have been calling to him over the air. The Duty Officer much regretted that he did not think he could help on this occasion except to suggest to his caller that he report his loss to the police and perhaps the Battersea Dog's Home, which welcomes strays.

A few evenings later, it was a cat-lover who caused a disturbance at 'Auntie's' headquarters. About 5.30, or, in log parlance 17.30, a Commissionaire ran into the 'Purser's' Office to announce: 'A woman has just rushed downstairs with a cat on her shoulder.'

Sensing the urgency, the Purser accompanied him quickly to the stairs, which they both rapidly descended to come face to face with the intruders in the sub-basement. They told the intruder that she must leave the building at once but she adamantly refused, shouting: 'Nobody's going to be unkind to my cat! Nobody!'

The angry woman proceeded to juggle unsuccessfully with a large bundle of letters that she had apparently addressed to various members of the BBC staff for reasons she would not disclose. Once more, she was asked to go quietly. Remaining defiant, she chose to squat down on the floor clutching her feline companion tightly to her bosom.

Finally reinforcements were summoned to eject woman and cat. The cat had its revenge, however; taking umbrage at this sudden manoeuvre, it fouled the uniform of one of their escorts on the way out.

Anyone bold enough to survey the ˉtight-rope dividing marital bliss and incompatible disaster would surely gain a little light relief from the substance of a call registered on 11 April 1977:

18.25 A Mrs Elizabeth Foyle rang to say that a friend had informed her that, in a News Summary during 'Woman's Hour', it had been reported that she had divorced her husband because he kept a lion in his garden. This was not true, she said. She had divorced her husband on grounds of cruelty, because he kept knocking her about. Instantly referring to the front page of the evening newspaper on his desk, the Duty Officer was able to inform Mrs Foyle that her divorce was clearly reported there, too, under the headline: 'THE LION ON THE LAWN KEPT HIS WIFE IN FEAR'. Instantly subdued by this information, Mrs Foyle said she would obtain a copy of the relevant journal and rang off.

The News Flash in 'Woman's Hour' had reported: 'An Essex woman got a divorce today on the grounds of cruelty. One of the complaints was that she was scared by the lion that her husband was keeping on his farm.'

Perhaps Mrs Foyle would have been less disturbed if the lion had belonged to a younger generation. One such proved a great attraction early in 1970 for a pretty raven-haired lady assistant in the Duty Office. Angela already had five cats which she doted on, cooking them special menus and taking them for walks in the meadows surrounding her country home in the heart of Buckinghamshire.

The lion cub, whose name was 'Jennie', had just been providing a natural roar in the basement studio for the producer of a disc-jockey programme, to whom this authentic sound was essential. She had been left in the corridor by her owner/trainer, who had dashed into the entrance hall for a moment to see the driver of the trailer which had transported Jennie to London from a zoo in Colwyn Bay. When Angela spotted the cub sitting on the carpet outside her office, she embraced Jennie with both arms, stroking and cuddling her as though she was one of her cats on the hearth at home. They were still sitting like this when the cub's owner came back to collect her. Turning pale, he instantly separated them; Jennie was almost six months old, an age when the cuddliest of cubs can turn dangerous and deliver a very nasty mauling.

As dusk was falling on the glorious, seemingly endless midsummer day of 1953, a soft June evening with magic abroad in the air, a hopeful American tourist rang the Duty Officer to ask him: 'Excuse me, sir, could you kindly tell me the best position I may take up in Berkeley Square tonight to hear the nightingale singing?'

Regrettably the unromantic Duty Officer of that night in Portland Place greatly disappointed the lady by doubting the bird's existence anywhere in the square. The late Eric Maschwitz, who wrote the heart-stirring song 'A Nightingale Sang in Berkeley Square' for an early wartime revue, *New Faces* (1939), would have relished that story as no doubt would any of his 'angels' still dining at the Ritz.

Bing Crosby with Pat Kirkwood

The nine-year-old Petula Clark

Jacqueline Wauters, mascot of the Free French

Cecil Madden Collection
General Eisenhower with Cecil Madden

Cecil Madden Collection
Jean Simmons in 'Variety Bandbox'

Cecil Madden Collection
Marlene Dietrich in the Queensberry Club

Muhammad Ali 'the Greatest' in the studio with Pete Murray

Danny Kaye with Peter Duncan, rehearsing for 'In Town Tonight'

Royal visit: HM King George VI, HM Queen Elizabeth and HRH Princess Elizabeth

Ariel photograph

Sea lion crossing the foyer, 6.30 am

The Duty Officer and Assistant take their share of eccentric calls, some from regulars, who tend to surface more often at the period of the full moon, which is clearly marked on their office calendar. These callers propagate many different kinds of lunacy.

Followers of the occult ring to propound their theories about the supernatural. Some peer into the future, some back into the past while others are content to discuss their visions of the present: 'Three times during the night, I saw a bright star shining above an oil rig in the North Sea. I am sure this was under the control of God.' No doubt he was right!

A memorable call for one Duty Officer came from a cheerful Cockney widow in Epsom, who, when moonlight became her, used to ring in for a friendly chat, usually about some News item that had either disturbed her or caught her fancy. On one night of the full moon, all in a few sentences, the old dear asked the Duty Officer to send her his photograph, invited him to marry her (it wasn't Leap Year!) before proposing a honeymoon trip on the Concorde.

'Oooh! You'd make me a lovely husband!' she cooed.

'Goodnight, Duckie!'

Provided our planet does not make a marked deviation from its apparently steady orbital course, it seems that British weather is likely to remain a permanent ice-breaker for the shy, the life-saving topic for introverts outside the media and extroverts within it. Bearing this in mind, it's not surprising that when, on 26 April 1976, the long-established format and times of the early-morning National Weather Forecast were changed, a sudden storm of protests caused the Duty Office staff (both of them) to reach for their raincoats and umbrellas. Their first forty-five callers complained in this fashion:

'Why on earth do you have to change the weather forecast times, which have remained static for so many years? Separate regional forecasts are no good to me because I travel about all over the country in my job. Temperatures and conditions change from one county to another, so I am always concerned about the state of the weather outside my region as well.'

'There is now no full forecast until one o'clock in the afternoon. This is a most unsatisfactory state of affairs.'

'I strongly object to the absence of detailed reports. When going out for the day, I don't know whether to take an umbrella or not.'

The wind of protest continued, sometimes at gale force. Said the President of an enthusiastic gliding club at Enstone, Oxfordshire:

Last Sunday, our club broke two records. The flight was made after listening to your 07.55 Weather Report, which we used as the basis upon which to plan our operation. Your wind details are vital to us gliders and we have come to depend on them. Please don't let us down!'

A mother of three had a half-term problem: 'I had planned to take the children to Whipsnade Zoo but had to cancel the outing because of the absence of a detailed weather forecast.'

Another middle-aged citizen complained: 'I'm not an old duffer, but in common with a good half of the country, I don't know whether 30 degrees Centigrade is hot or not!'

On the behalf of who knows how many Fahrenheit supporters, the late Patrick Hutber, City Editor of the *Sunday Telegraph* started a vigorous campaign. In his column on 19 June 1977, Mr Hutber wrote:

A fortnight ago, I quoted an assurance from Mr Douglas Muggeridge, Director of Programmes, Radio, that the BBC's policy was to give Fahrenheit after Centigrade where time allows. Since then, I have listened assiduously without hearing a single Fahrenheit reading given. Nor have my readers. What is more, those readers who rang the Weather Centre were told that Fahrenheit had been dropped at the BBC's request. On ringing the London Weather Centre, my own reporter was told that they (the BBC) have asked us to do it in Centigrade only.

On 3 July Mr Hutber wrote: 'I started this row because I believed that, if listeners wanted information in a particular form, they were entitled to have it.' He also wrote:

The BBC says: We must do our best for listeners, who will never get used to Centigrade, but they are not making much effort to do so.
    Fahrenheit is at present so rare on the air-waves that one reader sent me a telegram: 'Heard my first Fahrenheit on BBC Radio at 7.57 this morning.'

Two days later, the *Daily Mail* joined the fray with a Leader:

PLEASE TRANSLATE
It's up in the eighties again down in the South. Not for the BBC. They persist in giving the temperature in Centigrade, almost entirely disregarding Fahrenheit. For most people in this country, it's as if they were listening to a foreign-language station.

Mr Hutber continued his vigil, playing the BBC against the Weather Centre and vice versa throughout the summer. He had some support from MPs, who became just as irritated as the general public at being given temperatures they didn't understand. One wrote to the BBC's Director-General, who, according to Mr Hutber, replied that the Board of Governors have now ruled that Fahrenheit equivalents of Centigrade temperatures should be given frequently enough to provide the audience with adequate points of reference.
    The Director-General ended his letter (according to Mr Hutber): 'I hope your constituents will find the increase in Fahrenheit references helpful.'
    Nevertheless, Mr Hutber and his supporters continued to complain that they were still not hearing one temperature in two disclosed as Fahrenheit. Eventually, Hutber's Law showed results: In the *Sunday Telegraph* on 4 September he indicated that his hard-fought campaign had met with a fair measure of

success: 'I think we have very nearly won on Fahrenheit. Several times lately, I have heard intelligible temperatures dispensed with a more reasonable hand. The BBC have given in. The problem now is to keep the Weather Centre up to the mark.'

Another hardy annual principally enjoyed by the male sex in England is what the late Neville Cardus of cricketing fame once simply described in a Radio 4 broadcast as 'the summer game', which the West Indians prefer to call 'cricket, lovely cricket' as they chant their rhythmic calypsos on the stands.

Conversely, there are many Radio 3 listeners, who do not share this passion for the summer game. Quite simply, they prefer to listen to music. During the relay of the Centenary Test Match between England and India from Madras in January 1977, when music lovers were confined to VHF wavelengths, the Duty Office received no fewer than seventy calls before lunch on the first morning's play. The callers appeared to be allergic to bat and ball, completely uninterested in maiden overs. 'We have far too much of this sort of thing during the English season,' they protested as, indeed, they frequently do when any music programme is curtailed in favour of this native sport.

For *The Times* Cricket Correspondent, who reported this event from Madras, it was a joyous occasion. This is how he saw it under cloudless skies: 'Amid scenes of abundant goodwill here this morning, England won their first overseas series other than in New Zealand . . . They bowled India out in their second innings for 83, the lowest total ever made in a Test Match in India, which meant that England won the match by 200 runs and the Series with it.' However, very many calls of appreciation followed. Some even came from music lovers themselves. The most enthusiastic response came from a man who had cut himself during his morning shave. 'I was so excited at hearing this "live" commentary on the Test Match that my hand slipped and I cut my nose with my razor.'

In very cramped surroundings during the summer of 1975, the

experimental first-ever live broadcast was relayed from the House of Commons on 9 June. The 'ayes' and 'noes' from listeners, who proclaimed their verdict on this historic occasion, were literally fifty-fifty in their summing-up – half in favour, half against. Here are some of their comments:

'Extremely wonderful to hear this great initial broadcast from the Chamber.' 'So interesting and instructive. Marvellous radio!' 'How terribly interesting! I enjoyed it.' 'One of the most absorbing things I have ever heard on the air.' 'Absolutely fascinating. In fact, better than any "Afternoon Theatre".'

But there were those who missed their 'Afternoon Theatre' and said so:

'Very disappointed that we cannot have the Monday play as usual during the period of your Parliamentary experiment.' 'Much prefer listening to plays than to the monotonous proceedings in Parliament.'

One listener was worried about her ironing:

I always do my ironing on a Monday afternoon while listening to the play, and today feel quite desperate because I cannot concentrate while hearing the 'Monkey House'. I'm fed up with all that racket. I tell you, it has ruined my laundry!

Another listener considered the Parliamentary broadcast to be too noisy: 'What a din! Like a crowd of unruly schoolboys. I can't hear a word that's being said. How dare you cut "Woman's Hour" and make us lose our play.'

Yet another caller considered that the Paliamentary offering could be the possible alternative to a popular panel game: 'I suggest that today's broadcast from the House of Commons with the Right Honourable Gentlemen would make a good replacement for "Does The Team Think?".'

Following experimental broadcasts, new and fuller facilities were installed at Westminster in preparation for the historical day, 3 April 1978, when regular 'live' broadcasts during Question Time began. Again, Duty Office received complaints – nearly two hundred on the first afternoon. They followed a similar pattern to those of 1975, the majority again being listeners without the VHF waveband on which normal programmes were being transmitted. One woman telephoned from Manchester to say that she was so annoyed that Parliament was preventing her from listening to the normal afternoon fare that she intended to lobby her MP!

A hospital patient complained: 'Sets in hospitals are preselected. Patients are hardly likely to be aided in their recovery by listening to the rabble in the House of Commons.'

Other typical comments were:

I am furious to find these comedians at Westminster on medium wave instead of my usual programmes.'
'This wretched Parliamentary broadcasting constitutes a new form of mental cruelty.'
'I am missing the afternoon play and don't want to hear the "circus" from Westminster.'

However, as before, there were many who expressed their satisfaction at the new venture. They were not all students of politics and they were not all men. 'I greatly appreciate this new service. The Parliamentary broadcast brings the whole thing into perspective,' was the opinion of a woman in Baker Street, NW1.

A housewife in Teddington, Middlesex, telephoned to say: 'I was disappointed when your trial period of broadcasting from Westminster came to an end. Now I am delighted at the resumption. The commentary is excellent.'

A gentleman from Esher endorsed her remarks: 'Yes, carry on with Parliament. We like to know what they're up to.'

The words of popular songs occasionally come under fire. Listening to 'Top of the Pops' on 20 August 1976, a Surrey woman declared her revulsion at the lyrics of a song entitled: 'Heaven Is in the Back of a Cadillac'. She said: 'I'm sure it's not there.'

Another lyric to cause offence appeared in the broadcast of a revue *On the Fringe* on 20 August 1971, when fifty-two listeners rang to complain about the song: 'I'm giving up Men for Lent'. 'This is blasphemy,' they said. 'In any case, Lent ended five months ago.'

It was the tempo at which he heard a traditional song that annoyed a Londoner on 5 November 1972: 'I'm not a Yorkshireman myself, but I have a great respect for the inhabitants of that county and consider that the rendering of "Ilkley Moor Baht 'At" in swingtime is most improper and insulting to them.'

From orchestral noises to irregular noises in the sky. When, on 17 November 1976, Radio 2 Presenter John Dunn included in his evening programme a discussion of a current news story about strange noises in the stratosphere, the telephones in the Duty Room rang over sixty times in an hour and a quarter. These were some of the listeners' reactions:

'I hear wind and rumbling noises at four minutes past nine every night in Wantage, Oxfordshire.'

'We hear them at ten past nine in Exeter: "Rumble, bang, rumble." Last night, the vibrations were strong enough to loosen some tiles.'

'I live in Falmouth. I believe these are sonic booms made by the Concorde en route for Washington.'

'We hear these noises at ten minutes past nine on Thursdays in the Isle of Wight.'

'I am a coastguard and think that this is the Royal Navy at work.'

'Doors rattle every night. These strange booms make my hair stand on end.'

'We hear the exact noises described in Newquay, Scilly Isles, High Wycombe, Liphook, Hastings, Wimbledon, Folkestone and Bristol,' confirmed listeners in those areas.

A lady in Porlock, Somerset rang with a more specific experience:

I would like to mention that my family and friends began hearing these strange bangs about nine o'clock most nights

about twenty years ago. As children we were all frightened at
the noise, which we called 'the big gun'. I am now married
with an eight-year-old son, still live in the same place. The
sound has not changed throughout the years.

A caller from St Mary's in the Scilly Isles had yet another
theory about these nocturnal disturbances: 'I think they
possibly generate from an experimental aircraft base at Filton.'
Another listener, this time from the Isle of Wight, supported
the Concorde theory: 'These noises have only been heard over
here since regular Concorde flights began. I expect they are
carrying out "noise-reduction exercises".' John Dunn and the
Duty Office thought they must have succeeded because the
storm gradually abated and the calls ceased.

I first thought of writing this history of Broadcasting House
while I was working in the Duty Office – having occupied the
Purser's chair either full-time or part-time for nearly twenty
years, please forgive me if I look back with pleasure to some of
the memorable calls I personally received.

First Cuckoo

At breakfast-time on a beautiful spring morning in early April,
I received a cheerful call from a listener at Etchingham, East
Sussex. This lady was dithering with excitement in the manner
of that fluttering Variety artiste of the 1930s and '40s, Jeanne
de Casalis (alias 'Mrs Feather'). She had just heard the first
mellifluous notes of the cuckoo, and was anxious to broadcast
the fact.

'Cuckoo! Cuckoo!' she enthused. 'The cuckoo's calling.
Wait a minute. I've got a long extension . . .'

I waited patiently while she took her receiver on a long cable
out into her garden to point it directly at the tree in which the
cuckoo was perched.

'Cuckoo, cuckoo! cuckoo!' trilled the bird.

'Can you hear him?' she asked.

I responded that I could hear the bird's familiar notes loud
and clear.

I hope you are the right person for me to inform about this delightful event,' she said.

Mindful of the fact that for a long time '*The Times*' had appeared to appropriate this subject in their Letters to the Editor without actually owning the monopoly of the first cuckoo of spring, I replied: 'Yes, indeed, thank you very much. I will forward your glad tidings to the Newsroom.'

Fahrenheit

While Patrick Hutber was waging his Fahrenheit v. Centigrade campaign, a listener in New Malden vented her frustration at the absence of the Fahrenheit forecast.

'Duty Officer? . . . How do I know what to wear and tell the children what to wear? All the dresses in my wardrobe are hung under progressive Fahrenheit labels: 35F, 40F, 50F, 55F, 60F, 70F and so on.'

She did not understand the intricacies of the Centigrade system.

'I'm left housebound without a stitch to wear!' she cried. 'Without knowing the Fahrenheit temperature, I can't go out!'

Special Request

At dawn on 13 October 1976, I received an unexpected call from the Director-General's wife, Lady Curran, who asked me if I could arrange for Radio 2 disc jockey Terry Wogan to play a request for her husband, Sir Charles Curran, in celebration of his birthday. She said she would like Terry to ring her to discuss the secret offering.

During his next natural break in the studio, Terry phoned Lady Curran to find out what she had in mind. For him, it was a moment of trepidation with the fear that perhaps she was going to reprimand him for the occasional jocular references he made about the Director-General and his alleged 'frolics' on the roof of Broadcasting House in the early morning.

'Surely he doesn't listen to my rubbish?' said Terry.

'Oh, yes, he does,' replied Lady Curran. 'He adores it. Do please play a birthday request for him: anything you can find by his favourite composer, Mozart. By the way, he is in the shower at the moment. Please play it in ten minutes' time if you can.'

Terry complied with Lady Curran's request by spinning the most appropriate Mozart disc he could summon from the Gramophone Library, accompanied by his good wishes for the birthday.

The reprimand came from the Director-General himself two days later: 'What an incorrigible pair of schemers you and my wife are!' Then, in the very next sentence he changed his tune: 'Thank you very much for remembering my birthday and for the record you played for me. I always enjoy your programme.'

Spoonerisms

During one broadcast of the popular quotation game 'Quote – Unquote', Arthur Marshall quoted the Reverend Spooner, Warden of New College, Oxford in the nineteenth Century as having said: 'You've tasted a whole worm!' A bright student rang to say that while this quotation was correct it was also incomplete. 'The whole quote', he advised, 'can be found in the Encyclopedia Britannica, 1919 Edition:

Addressing a delinquent undergraduate, the Reverend Spooner exclaimed: 'You have tasted two whole worms; you have hissed all my mystery lectures and been caught fighting a liar in the quad; you will leave Oxford by the next town drain!'

Victor

On 20 September 1977, an African quadruped with spotted skin, long neck and legs captured the anxiety and imagination of the animal-loving public. He was a giraffe named Victor.

Victor was the proud possessor of three wives, bearing the entieing names of Domino, Dribbles and Arabesque. It was during his last amorous encounter with Arabesque that the fifteen-year-old giraffe had the grave misfortune to do the 'splits'.

After his sudden parting from Arabesque, the giraffe sank to ground level and remained there immobilized for almost a week, during which time the Broadcasting House switchboard and the Purser's office were the recipients of a stream of telephone calls from well-wishers, some of whom asked if there was an address to which they could send 'Get Well Soon' cards.

The many who offered serious suggestions for remedies to bring Victor back to mobility included a masseuse in New York: 'Shovel the ground away underneath Victor, then slide a tarpaulin under him before lifting him upwards.'

Some advocated a plastic bath being put under Victor to take all his weight: 'Fill it with water, then let him float to the top.'

A further suggestion was offered by the British Waterways Board, who suggested using their pneumatic fending: if passed underneath Victor, it could be pumped up in order to raise him placidly to the upright position.

A physiotherapist rang to say that her bull-dog had suffered a similar indignity, but had responded very well to electrical treatment. 'Perhaps Victor would do likewise?'

The vigil continued at Marwell Zoo until the early afternoon of 20 September when Victor, one ton in weight and 18 feet 6 inches tall, was winched to his feet in a set of canvas trousers provided by the Royal Navy in Portsmouth. Sadly, all the stress and strain had taken their toll of poor Victor, who expired twenty minutes later. He died bravely with his head buried in the arms of his devoted keeper, Ruth Giles.

During Victor's final hours, anxious listeners continued to ring Broadcasting House, eager to hear the latest bulletin. After his death had been announced in a News Flash, one grief-stricken woman told me: 'I think there will be as much mourning for Victor as there was for Elvis Presley.' She was right.

Wimbledon

Probably the zaniest conversation I ever had with a member of the vast listening public occurred on a hot July afternoon in

1975, during the live television relay of the Ladies Singles Final at Wimbledon between the formidable Billy Jean King and Yvonne Cawley (née Goolagong).

The already tense atmosphere prevailing on the Centre Court was being further aggravated by a helicopter, buzzing low over the arena, emitting a sufficient number of decibels to force the umpire to decree a temporary cessation of play. While the offending machine was drifting slowly westwards, I answered a call from an irate middle-aged TV spectator mouthing a strong Cockney accent. His opening gambit was: 'Can't you get that bleedin' 'elicopter aht of the sky?' I replied that the BBC were not responsible for the flight paths over Wimbledon, but assured him that play would shortly resume. Meanwhile the lady finalists kept their cool on their respective sides of the net, but the zealous Cockney retained his impatience.

He served me an ace: 'GET IT AHT OF THE SKY!' he thundered. 'Surely you can get it dahn aht of the bleedin' sky?'

I again tried to explain that BBC had no control over this particular flight path, suggesting he address his grievance to the Air Ministry. The overheated viewer would not be assuaged, so the conversation continued, our final rally being:

DUTY OFFICER1: Why don't you ring the Air Ministry?
COCKNEY: 'Why don't *you* phone the BBC!!!

DEUCE

All telephone calls reach the Purser's Office via the BBC's private telephone exchange, which now operates with an electronic DDI (Direct Dialling In) system – this has slightly reduced the staff needed, to thirty regular telephonists, who work night and day shifts, and six supervisors. They transfer routine and emergency calls, and listeners' complaints, to the Duty Officer.

Outstanding news has always affected the BBC telephone exchange whether at a time of celebration or disaster. When the Duke and Duchess of Kent were married, thousands of listeners wanted to know in advance what she would wear.

In the Reithian era, it was said that nobody on the ship had a greater respect for the exchange and its cheerful efficiency than the first Director-General. He was very proud of this service, admitting that he himself was one of their most exacting customers. Once he had given the number of a business call, either home or abroad, he expected it to be noted, so that if he ever wanted it again, no matter how long afterwards, all he needed to say was, 'Please get Mr So-and-so' to be connected.

One of the best-loved supervisors, now retired, a lively brunette with a delightful sense of humour that befits an Irish lass, was Eileen O'Sullivan, who in wartime served in the WRNS. In Eileen's experience, the impact on the switchboard made by the assassination of President John F. Kennedy on 22 November 1963, has never been capped. She remembers Radio Newsreel being interrupted by a newsflash. On this terrible day, Eileen heard the shattering news at home. She listened, frozen with horror, wondering how her friend and deputy, Ann Howard, who had just been promoted to supervisor, was coping.

The following day, Ann revealed to her that she and her accompanying operators had almost worked themselves to a standstill. Expatriate Americans who could not get lines to the USA rang the BBC from all over the world crying and pleading that the news must not be true. She said it was a heart-rending exhausting night. The calls were never-ending. More than a thousand were handled and no one took a meal break.

The death of Grace Archer has been described earlier. Said Eileen:

I doubt very much if the original Archers fans ever forgave that particular scriptwriter for terminating the life of Grace Archer. A number of people rang up to make sure that it was the character in the serial and not the actress playing her who had died. The majority called to protest that this particular incident was quite unnecessary, also in extremely bad taste.

Of the individual listeners who telephoned, one man said that he had had to call a doctor because his mother had suffered a heart attack, while another man was distraught since his wife, who was pregnant, had collapsed in hysterics.

However, Eileen has many lighter, happier recollections. During one edition of 'Panorama', the late Richard Dimbleby hoodwinked viewers by showing a mock spaghetti harvest in Italy. Some viewers were actually taken in, while others strongly disagreed that spaghetti grew on trees and angrily said so. In fact, the date was 1 April.

One evening she was approached by an operator who asked her what she should do with a call for 'The Beatles'. Without hesitation, she told her to tell the caller to ring BBC Bristol and ask for the Natural History Unit. 'They know all about beetles,' advised Eileen. Little did she realize that this was the beginning of a new age of popular music – often the bane of a BBC switchboard operator's life.

Another story about the Beatles comes from the day when the announcer reading the one o'clock News told listeners that Ringo Starr was quite comfortable in hospital after having his 'toenails' out! He naturally meant 'tonsils' and, during the ensuing avalanche of calls, Eileen spoke to one matey lady, who said in very clipped tones: 'I say, m'dear, awfully easy mistake to make, y'know . . . same shorthand outline, but he missed out the circle . . . could happen to anyone.'

One afternoon, a dear old lady rang to say to Eileen: "'Ere, you know that cat, Sailor, wot's got lost from Mrs Dale's Diary? Well, he's bin in our garden several times, I see'd 'im.'

Very late one night, a slurred voice said: 'I shay, ish that Old Auntie BBC?' Eileen retorted: 'This *is* Auntie speaking personally.'

All she heard then was a loud hiccup, a clatter and a thud. For some time afterwards, she wondered if the man had hurt himself and if he ever recovered!

CHAPTER SEVEN

Quaecunque

THE BOOKSHELF IN THE Duty Office contains a priceless tome, its gilt-edged pages strongly bound in handsome black leather and weighing eight and a half pounds. The front cover displays the BBC coat of arms, delicately inscribed in gold leaf with the Latin caption *Quaecunque* ('Whatsoever things').

Quaecunque superseded the original BBC motto ('Nation Shall Speak Peace unto Nation', which was originally suggested by one of the first five Governors of the Corporation, Dr Rendall) and was taken from Dr Rendall's Latin inscription – later translated into English by Sir Roger Carey – in the Entrance Hall of Broadcasting House, partly based upon a passage from Philippians IV: 'Whatsoever things are beautiful and honest and of good report . . .'

The 250 pages of this unique Visitors' Book – now mostly filled – contain the signatures of several thousand famous persons including monarchs, princes, princesses, prime ministers, cabinet ministers, MPs, servicemen, authors, authoresses, actors, actresses, musicians, journalists – in fact all categories of broadcasters who have been invited to the 'Wardroom', firstly in Savoy Hill, then in Broadcasting House during the six decades since the wireless began.

Page One is headed, on 4 February 1926, by the signature of the Duke of Portland – it ends with a delightful pen and ink self-portrait by one of the most popular music-hall stars of all time, Harry Lauder.

The first thirty-three pages of the book, inscribed during 'Auntie's' residence at Savoy Hill, are filled with the signatures of 436 celebrities who broadcast between 1926 and 1932, those exciting nursery days of the wireless when owners of crystal sets were spellbound by the magic they heard through their headphones.

July 7th 1932

Visit of
Their Majesties
The King and Queen

George R.I.

Mary R.

4.3.26   Portland

Winifred Portland

17/2/26   Edward German

17/2/26   Marie Belloc Lowndes
2/3/26   G. K. A. Bell
6/3/26   Jno Galsworthy

March 6. 1926

The first visitor on page five, Viscountess Nancy Astor, was immediately followed by Joe Childs (jockey to King George V). Lower down the page the eye catches Sir Walford Davies (conductor) and Pouishnoff, the Russian pianist. They were closely followed by Robert Baden-Powell, founder of the Boy Scouts Association. Edward, Prince of Wales makes his first entry in the book on the glorious first of June 1927 heading page 17. Page 18 is headed by the conductor and composer Thomas Beecham, joined a few semi-breves later by Sir Henry J. Wood – instigator of the now traditional Promenade Concerts.

A welcome visitor in the spring of 1928, the Rt. Hon. Winston S. Churchill, was very soon followed by the Rt. Hon. Neville Chamberlain whom fate decreed that Churchill should follow into No. 10 Downing Street when Britain went to war eleven years later.

Page 25 is headed by Megan Lloyd George closely pursued by Sir Henry Newbolt, the Rt. Hon. John Simon and the Rt. Hon. Ramsay MacDonald who was later to become the first Labour Prime Minister of England.

Page 26 reveals the most important name in the book: the name without whose presence on the earth none of the other signatures would have appeared at the time they did. It is that of 'Mr Wireless' himself, Marchese Guglielmo Marconi, whose bold underlined signature would surely be of interest to any calligrapher. Sharing the same page are the noted English historian, G.M. Trevelyan, and J.M. Keynes whose radical ideas were soon to pervade the economy.

Names that catch the eye on page 28, in addition to the Prince of Wales, are the Rt. Hon. Stanley Baldwin and Sir William Beveridge, instigator of the Welfare State, and Lord Beaverbrook.

The last celebrity to sign the book at Savoy Hill was the French film director, René Clair, who had already set his seal on a successful career with box-office hits such as *Paris qui dort*, *Entr'acte*, *An Italian Straw Hat* and *A Nous La Liberté*. He will always be best remembered by the film to which he refers in his entry thus:

Mes meilleurs voeux
en souvenir de Sous les Toits de Paris
Savoy Hill.

Page 35, the first to be filled following 'Auntie's" move to Portland Place, includes the autographs of Charles B. Cochrane ('Cockie', the flamboyant impresario of the 1930s and early 1940s, whose 'Young Ladies' were equally delectable both on stage and at the stage door); Rt. Hon. Stanley Baldwin MP., Rt. Hon. Kingsley Wood, Rt. Hon. H. Graham White (Visiting politicians), Dorothy L. Sayers (novelist and play-wright).

The first Royal visit to the BBC's new headquarters was made by King George V and Queen Mary on 7 July 1932, the first occasion upon which the Royal Standard was flown over Broadcasting House.

The briefing was that no one should be admitted into the Main Hall after 2.30 p.m.; that no staff on duty be allowed to smoke between 3.00 and 5.00 p.m.; that ordinary clothes were to be worn except by those accompanying the Royal Party and by those presented to them, who were instructed to wear morning dress. The Director of Programmes was responsible for arranging for an orchestra to be on stage in the Concert Hall. Staff attending the ceremony were told to be seated there in the same formation as that adopted when the DG had addressed them in May, – that is, men in the centre block, women in the two wing blocks. The floor of the Hall had to be completely filled before the gallery was used.

Upon their arrival, the King and Queen were immediately escorted to the Concert Hall by Mr Chilman. As they entered, staff and orchestra rose. Their Majesties walked to the centre of the Hall as the orchestra played one verse of the National Anthem, sung by all. The traditional three cheers followed.

King George V and Queen Mary visited the Vaudeville, Chamber Music and Dance Music studios. They listened to the Wireless Singers, the BBC Dance Orchestra and Military Band.

Roger Eckersley, Director of Entertainments survived a slightly embarrassing experience when, after being presented to the Queen he was addressed by her at the official luncheon.

'I don't know why I should have been shy,' said Eckersley, 'no one could have been kinder or more patient than Queen Mary with my endeavours to explain things. However, I felt that I had not been much of a success. When I confessed this afterwards to a friend, who had been sitting at the next table, he replied: 'I am not surprised. Why did you persist in calling the Queen "my dear"?'

The Royal guests were shown how the varied episodes of a drama production were co-ordinated. They also visited the Effects Studio before taking tea in the Director-General's office.

March 1936 is highlighted by the visit of King Edward VIII on the first day of the month: it must have been one of the very few times that he wrote his signature in a visitors' book during his brief term as monarch.

When King George VI and Queen Elizabeth, accompanied by their two daughters, Princess Elizabeth and Princess Margaret, visited Broadcasting House (13 March 1939) they entered the small basement studios (BB) soon after a 'Toy Town' story dealing with the 'Disgraceful Business at Mrs Goose's' had started in Children's Hour. The Princesses, wearing dove-grey coats and grey berets, were highly amused by the quavering voice of Larry the Lamb (Ewart Scott) and the guttural English of Denis the Dachshund (Norman Shelley).

In a fourth-floor studio, a record was made of the general conversation, in which the Royal Party took part. Later, they listened to a reproduction of this over a loudspeaker.

The Royal visit to mark the Corporation's Jubilee Year was a night of nights at Broadcasting House, on 5 December 1947, when King George VI and Queen Elizabeth with Princess Margaret visited various studios to see certain programmes being broadcast. They spoke to about a hundred staff during their three-hour visit. Office boys and messenger girls, lucky in the ballot for seats in the Concert Hall, had places which senior officials would have given anything for.

There was a Command Performance of the King's favourite Variety prgramme 'ITMA', after which the Royal Party spent a quarter of an hour chatting to Tommy Handley and Company.

Two of Tommy Handley's jokes during the Royal visit are

recorded in Archives: 'The Radio Doctor kept a cupboard of pink pills, which he eats at lunchtime,' and 'Some announcers play records backwards – Day Fine One, from Fly Butter Madame.'

Turning on through the passing years and decades, one's attention is arrested here and there by a particular page shared by a number of memorable names. One such is page 94 which was headed by the accomplished and dearly loved actor Robert Donat. Other eminent signatures on the same page include: Ambrose Fleming, the scientist who pioneered the application of electricity to lighting and heating on a large scale; Gordon Richards, many times Champion Jockey from 1925; Henry Wood, instigator of the cherished Promenade Concerts; Alan Cobham, aviation pioneer of 'Flying Circus' fame and Norman Birkett, the renowned QC.

Into the next decade and on to page 107, which probably houses within the space of twenty days one of the most remarkable lists of autographs ever to appear in one Visitors' Book. General Charles de Gaulle heads the scroll, closely followed by Lord Woolton, Minister of Food in the Second World War.

A few days later came R.A. Butler, Under Secretary of State for Foreign Affairs; Duff Cooper, Lord of the Admiralty; William Somerset Maugham; Philip Noel-Baker, advocate of the League of Nations; 'The Master' – that is to say the 'bitter sweet' but unforgettable Noël Coward; and the actor who was topping the cinema box-office opinion polls when the Second World War began, Leslie Howard, who disappeared in 1943 in mysterious circumstances; he is said to have been engaged on a secret mission, and unconfirmed reports allege that the aircraft in which he was travelling from Lisbon had been shot down by a German plane, in the erroneous belief that Winston Churchill was among the passengers.

Page 116 is of particular interest because it includes the entourage of Tafari Haile Selassie, Emperor of Abyssinia, together with HIR Princess of Ethiopia and Zawde Gebre Selassie. They helped to make the Langham Hotel opposite Broadcasting House fashionable in the 1930s.

In his role as the first Duty Officer, Peter Montgomery entertained many foreign potentates in the 'wardroom' – one of his earliest encounters being with Charles de Gaulle who, as mentioned in an earlier chapter, was a frequent wartime visitor. Peter recalls the General's initial visit to Broadcasting House in June 1940:

A tall saturnine figure, haggard with lack of sleep and anxiety, newly arrived from France whence he had escaped that morning to try and rally his scattered and demoralized forces from a new headquarters in London. He had entered the building unnoticed, and I happened to be the first to encounter him in the foyer.

'Je suis de Gaulle,' he said.

It was difficult to know what to say in return, especially as the General spoke little English and my French was equally restricted. However, I was immediately able to contact Sir Stephen Tallents, then Controller of Overseas Broadcasting, and they were able to get down to business together.

Shortly afterwards, on 18 June 1940, the day that Italy declared war on France and Britain, General de Gaulle was able to address his compatriots: 'Whatever happens, the flame of French resistance must not and shall not die.'

Up till then, it had been Darsie Gillie, British News Editor in charge of the French section, who had addressed the people of Occupied France. A team of 'free' French supplied the programme 'Ici la France', which was a vital wartime overseas broadcast. The teams was competently led by the renowned Actor/Producer, Michael Saint Denis, who acquired the fictitious name of Jacques Duchesne. He had come to Broadcasting House after landing at Weymouth as a refugee.

A more fraught occasion recalled by Peter Montgomery was the first visit by the Queen of Holland:

I remember one frosty morning when Queen Wilhelmina was due to come to BH to speak to her people. I was descending the staircase to the front hall to check that all was in readiness for her arrival when, to my horror, I saw her car already drawn up outside – at least ten minutes early. At the same moment I noticed with additional dismay that the Home Guard, which was in the habit of turning out guards of honour on such occasions, was in a terrible state of unreadiness – some tightening their braces, others fastening their gaiters – and all clearly not knowing whether they were coming or going. However, the Queen, with consummate tact, sailed in looking the other way as she passed quickly through the hall and into the lift that bore her and her lady-in-waiting to the safety of the studio above.

Duty Officer Colonel Forty records:

A Danish conductor, Mogens Woldike, brought many leading Danes to BH on February 22nd, 1948 to listen to a concert on the Third Programme. They, including the Danish Ambassador, were entertained upstairs by the Head of Music: at 9.30 p.m. Duty Room was asked to arrange transport to take the Ambassador to his home.

His wife kept the car waiting twenty minutes in a vain search for her gloves. This was rather a nuisance as we needed it very soon for General Bor (a Polish General), but luckily his wife had also lost some of her clothing: a search for her left boot proceeded vigorously and I'm glad to say met with success.

On the evening of 3 May the same year, Forty had to entertain Bertrand Russell and Kingsley Martin. He logged:

Verbal strife broke out between Bertrand Russell and Kingsley Martin, in which BR said: 'Of all the tyrannies of history the Kremlin was by far the worst, the most cruel, the most efficient, and the greatest danger.'

Kingsley Martin, chuntering over his pipe, said: 'Bertie, that is the first time I have ever known you speak like an old man. That was a Tory speech.'

Russell replied: 'I can't stand you, Kingsley. You are completely insincere.'

BR then got up and walked out, after which there was rather a silence.

Forty also recalls:

On another occasion a well-known politician with a puckish sense of humour came into Duty Room while I was dealing with an enquiry from a lady: I put the telephone down to look for some information. Being left standing on his own, the ubiquitous MP could not resist picking up the receiver; in soothing tones he murmured: 'It's all right, Madam, we are just getting the information for you. Hold on please, the Duty Officer will be with you in a moment.' The caller would have been very surprised had she known that the second speaker at our end was George Brown of Belper – later to become Foreign Secretary in Harold Wilson's government.

On the evening of 29 April 1949 M. René Massigli, the French Ambassador, presented to the BBC on behalf of the Government of France, a magnificent modern tapestry 'in recognition of the help and comfort the London radio offered in the dark days of the occupation'. The tapestry was specially created by the famous French designer Lurcat, and depicts in the feathery and leafy style so characteristic of his work a poet drawing inspiration from the scenery around him. 'All this,' the Ambassador said, 'would not have been possible without the generosity with which the BBC put its technical facilities and its staff at the disposal of French patriots in England.'

In presenting the tapestry to Lord Simon, Chairman of the BBC Governors, the Ambassador recalled the work of Jacques Duchesne, Jean Oberle and Pierre Bourdon; also that of Mr Darsie Gillie, then Paris correspondent of the *Manchester Guardian*. He spoke too of the messages of Mr Churchill, whose French was thought to be moving but 'highly individual'. Lord Simon replied that the work done by the BBC had been made possible by the way in which the staff had used these advantages. Director-General Wir William Hayley supported Lord Simon eloquently, speaking the French language. The Lurcat tapestry is still admired by visitors to Broadcasting House today.

A much later Duty Officer, Frank Cobb, has different reminiscences:

An African chief arrived one day with five of the seventy-five children he claimed to have in his family. Discussing differences in social customs, he remarked with a broad grin: 'I always take boiling water with my champagne!' He then asked a colleague on duty that day how many children he had. 'Five' was the answer.

The Chief beamed as he replied: 'Keep on trying, then you may have as many as I've got!'

For broadcasting in the 1950s, who better to open the batting than Denis Compton, the Middlesex and England cricketer: he shared page 171 in the Visitors' Book with, among others: David Low, celebrated *Evening Standard* cartoonist; Cyril Ray, journalist; Fred Hoyle, astronomer, and Michael Wilding and David Niven, film stars.

One only has to turn another page to find Bing Crosby and Bob Hope's delectable *Road* companion, Dorothy Lamour. Other show-business personalities to share this page are Gladys Cooper, Anton Dolin, Gladys Young, Joyce Barbour and Wilfred Pickles.

On 7 October 1950, Duty Room was made brighter by the glowing presence of the Trapp Family Singers. Their experiences under the shadow of the Gestapo in Austria at the outbreak of the Second World War formed the basis for one of the most successful musicals ever to be presented on either stage or screen – *The Sound of Music*.

Carry on turning the pages and the attention is quickly arrested by the names Jack (Dixon of Dock Green) Warner, Harriet Cohen, the noted concert pianist, the Surrey and England cricketers Eric and Alec Bedser, film stars Bette Davis and Charles Boyer – not forgetting Hollywood's legendary 'tough guy' Humphrey Bogart, and a host of other celebrities too numerous to mention here.

All the autographs in 'Auntie's' Visitors' Book except two were written in blue-coloured ink. One of the two exceptions was Harold Wilson. He signed in red!

When King George VI and Queen Elizabeth visited Broadcasting House on 4 December 1947, John Snagge, who was then Head of Presentation for the Home Service, provided a gold pen for them to sign the Visitors' Book. Shortly afterwards this pen was anonymously presented to the Corporation by the staff announcers as an appreciation of their responsibilities on that day. It was suitably engraved to mark the occasion of the Royal visit in the Silver Jubilee year of the BBC. This pen has been further inscribed to record subsequent visits made by royalty to BBC premises.

On 27 March 1943 the Paisley edition of the *Daily Express* recalled an early wartime visit by Winston Churchill to Broadcasting House:

A short while after he became Prime Minister, Winston Churchill visited some friends in the west side of London. He was scheduled to address the nation that evening. It was already dark when he left and he feared that he might be late for the broadcast. Running over to a cab that was parked at the kerb, he told the driver to take him to the Broadcasting Station.

'Sorry, but I can't take you that far,' said the cabby, not recognizing his distinguished fare.

'Why not?' asked the PM.

'Mr Churchill is broadcasting in a little while – I'm going home to tune in. I wouldn't miss his speech for the world.'

The great statesman was so flattered by this that he handed the man a £1 note. At the sight of this the driver's eyes almost popped out of his head.

'Hop right in!' he said, starting the motor, 'Churchill ain't that important!'

Among the many hundreds of guests whom I have personally welcomed during my tour of duty in the 'wardroom' I particularly remember the following.

Lord 'Manny' Shinwell, that grand old humour-loving stalwart of the Labour Party, who came into the Duty Room with Frank Gillard – then recently retired Home Service Chief – who was producing him in a Current Affairs programme that day. Lord Shinwell had not long celebrated his ninetieth birthday.

'May I leave Lord Shinwell with you while I go down to line things up in the studio?' Gillard asked.

'Certainly,' I said, shaking hands with the venerable politician, who swiftly diverted his eye-line from the cocktail cabinet to his departing producer, calling after him:

'I see. You are going down to the operating theatre leaving me to take the anaesthetic!'

Shortly before receiving the Rt. Hon. Edward Heath on the night of 15 December 1975, I had been reading Andrew Roth's biography of the Prime Minister in the previous Conservative Government. Roth revealed that when Heath was Chief Whip he was stricken with jaundice:

> The immediate impact of the jaundice was to make the drinking of alcoholic beverages impossible initially. After a while he was told that he could drink champagne in moderation. Later he was informed that malt whisky was purer than blended. For many years thereafter he stuck to a single malt whisky.

I was given so little notice of the Rt. Honourable Gentleman's impending visit that I did not have time to procure a bottle of Highland malt to suit his taste. When asking him what he would like for refreshment, I was well prepared for the statesman's reply:

'Have you any Highland Malt?'

'Very sorry, sir, only a proprietary brand I'm afraid.'

'All part of the economy drive, I suppose,' Mr. Heath retorted. I poured him a blended whisky and was pleased to note that he appeared to enjoy it.

Few who work in Broadcasting House in the daytime are privileged to, or even have the time to, take a bath. However, this facility was offered to and was much enjoyed by a temperamental marine visitor, whose loud bark awoke me at first light one glorious morning during the July heatwave of 1976: it was a sea lion.

The mammal was appearing in the flipper-prints of a former member of his species to re-enact a scene that was filmed forty years before for an experimental television programme. This one was far from docile. It had entered Broadcasting House at 4.30 a.m. quietly enough, accompanied by its handler, but later, when doing some strenuous filming in a nearby mews, it became over-heated and ran down the main street closely pursued by the film unit.

Two ploys were used to calm the sea lion. Firstly, the lure of a bucketful of sprats, secondly an invigorating splash around in the ladies' sub-basement bathroom. The sea lion waddled contentedly down the stairs and dived happily into the already prepared bath. It barked, shook its fins, then found the plug, which it quickly removed – often. As the bath ran dry, the frustrated attendant had to refill it again and again! Fortunately, at this stage of the drought, which had just been officially declared in some parts during one of the hottest summers of the century, water restrictions had not yet been imposed in London even for sea lions.

On the afternoon before the 1977 Grand National Richard Pitman – who later became paddock commentator with the BBC Television Racing Team after his retirement as first jockey to the highly successful National Hunt trainer Fred Winter – came into the wardroom before being interviewed on 'Woman's Hour',. History was about to be made in the next day's running of the greatest steeplechase: Charlotte Brew, the

30 March 1977

*I only hope that Charlotte Brew
doesn't burn her bra after the 1977
Grand National*

Richard Pitman —

first woman to have a mount in the National, was entered to ride her own twelve-year-old gelding Barony Fort. Richard's comment, reproduced above, was hardly complimentary or encouraging to this courageous pioneer. However, Charlotte did her sex credit by jumping twenty-six of the thirty fences before Barony Fort refused at the twenty-seventh obstacle.

One celebrity whom I several times welcomed into the wardroom was the world's favourite crooner, Harry Lillie ('Bing') Crosby. When Bing strolled nonchalantly into Duty Room after finishing a guest broadcast with Pete Murray one unusually bright warm morning in February, I asked him if he was going to enjoy a round of golf. He shook his head sadly. 'I'd love a game but your gloomy weather prophets told me that you normally have nothing better to offer than rain, snow, ice or fog here this month. So I didn't bring my clubs.' I offered to lend him mine but he said regretfully that he had agreed to do extra recording sessions, which would now occupy all his time.

On Bing Crosby's last visit to Broadcasting House on 15 September 1977, just before his unforgettable family show at the London Palladium, he was again principal guest in Pete

Murray's 'Open House' on Radio Two. This time, he was accompanied by his charming wife, Kathryn. To borrow an American expression, the show was a real 'humdinger'. It could hardly have been anything else.

Uncannily, the first of Bing's records played on his last programme, chosen by the 'Groaner' himself, was entitled 'The Only Way to Go':

> It's the only way to go
> The only way I know
> We'll be happy till we die
> My foolish dreams and I . . .

Less than a month after that broadcast, Bing reached the end of the road as the great Harry Lauder had done many years before him. Bing collapsed with a heart attack after walking to the clubhouse from the eighteenth green on a golf course near Madrid. One of his partners, Spanish professional Valentin Barrios, told the press: 'Bing had shown no signs of fatigue. He was happy and carefree, singing as he went round the course', while Kathryn Crosby was reported as saying: 'I can't think of any better way for a golfer who sings for a living to finish the round.'

For Bing Crosby, King of Crooners, it was surely the best – perhaps the only – way to go, but for me, who'd seen him so recently, the news of his death came as a great shock.

CHAPTER EIGHT

Anchors Aweigh

EARLY ON A DEWY June morning in 1986, I moored opposite a parking meter on the port side of the ship as the blue of the night was meeting the golden haze of the day. I absorbed the scene that more than fifty years ago had enraptured Michael Carr's playboy in 'Regent Street Rhapsody'.

I had not emerged from a nightclub but had driven at break of dawn from Epsom Downs to keep a date with the Radio Two DJ Ray Moore. After watching him putting out his lively programme across the nation – 'Always a good little earner,' he says – we ascended to the restaurant on the eighth floor, where 300 breakfasts and 800 lunches are served daily.

In this particular BBC restaurant, a catering assistant once managed to go through a whole lunchtime service with two large lettuce leaves pinned to her ears while serving customers. When the manager spotted her aural salad and asked the reason for this decoration, she said it was to relieve her headache!

A more disturbing incident occurred at a time when a drama production required twenty actors to be made up as lepers. As they looked so unpleasant, it was requested that lunch should be sent to them in the studio each day. One day, the restaurant staff forgot to deliver, so the actors came up into the studio seeking their meal. Within minutes the restaurant had cleared: it was completely empty except for the leprous actors.

A well-known DJ, who used to attend the restaurant regularly, always cracked a joke with the ladies behind the counter. One day, he said to his favourite server: 'Hello, darling, when are you going to make love to me?' Straight-faced, the blonde maiden replied: 'Will 4.30 do?'

Over the bacon and eggs and the renowned BBC coffee, Ray Moore told me that Broadcasting House has always had a profound influence on his life:

It is without doubt my favourite building in all the world. I remember on VE day as a sickly child, I was not allowed out to the street parties. A prisoner indoors, I used to listen to the news read by Alvar Lidell. I knew in those moments that Broadcasting House was my spiritual home. I desperately wanted to be on the radio, to work in Broadcasting House. I knew I had to be there.

Back in the spring of 1962, as an impoverished out of work actor living in a drunken-down bordello near Marble Arch, I secured the treasured position as an assistant in a cigarette shop. This Dickensian establishment was in Regent Street, near to Broadcasting House, which I used to visit at lunchtimes. I used to sit by the bookshop watching the comings and goings of various broadcasters, hoping maybe I would catch a glimpse of Franklin Engelmann, Michael Brooke, or any of my heroes.

I eventually arrived as a BBC Staff Announcer in Broadcasting House in 1967. At that time my immediate boss was John Snagge, with Andrew Timothy and David Lloyd-James in tow. Also on the strength were such luminaries as Alvar Lidell, Roy Williamson, Douglas Smith and Bruce Wyndham. Our Announcers' meetings were then held in the Council Chamber. To a young novice like me these learned gatherings were hallowed reverential occasions, all conducted under the stern gaze of the bust of my messianic hero, Lord Reith.

In the office, there hung a strange, haunting painting: I coveted it the moment I saw it. It was painted by an old BBC hand during the height of the Second World War. It depicted Broadcasting House as a staunch shadowy Shape against the impenetrable darkness of the blackout, pierced only by a couple of searchlights. Almost totally black but utterly moving, it spoke volumes to me. I discovered it to be John Snagge's personal property. After a deal of arm-twisting and grovelling, John reluctantly agreed to let me have it on the payment of £20 to a charity. It is one of my treasured possessions. To this day, it hangs in my hall.

Returning to the hall below, I encountered the Senior House Foreman of Central Services, Phil Scott, the Mr Chilman of the 1980s. His robust, portly, nineteen-stone figure provides a definite air of security to the hall as one enters. His cheerful countenance and eagerness to help are always apparent, much appreciated by staff and visitors alike.

Phil served in the Royal Navy as a Bosun's mate on a destroyer in the Pacific during the war against Japan from 1942 to 1946. He joined the BBC in 1947.

Discipline then, more than now, was very much like naval discipline amongst the uniformed staff. Walking along the corridors, I imagined myself patrolling the companionways of a large liner. The House Engineers area and the Boiler House strongly resembled the Navy, in which most of the original stokers served.

Owing to the vastness of the organization compared with Mr Chilman's time, there are now Staff Units, Staff Records and House Managers, who look after the purse strings, while my mates and I do the actual work that Mr Chilman did in his time.

Phil finds the voyage more turbulent now because there are more crises and the security is greater. A few years back, he was involved in the 'Poisoned Mars Bars' episode when an Anti-Hunting Group infected chocolate-coated bars and delivered some to various places, including Broadcasting House. 'After receiving a telephone call to say that the poisoned packet had been delivered, we handed it to the police, who carried out their investigation.'

Phil also has a story about the Rt. Hon. George Brown, MP for Belper. 'After a general election, he walked out of the studio where he was being interviewed by Robin Day, who had upset him. He eventually calmed down but had to be coaxed to return to the microphone. This sort of thing happens and we must keep an eye on it.'

Far more troublesome to Phil Scott and his crew were the screaming pop fans in the heyday of the Osmonds and the Bay City Rollers. The fans of the latter, labelled 'teeny-boppers', were about twelve years old and violent. Their language was violent as well. They used to come in their hordes. One night the area around Broadcasting House was blocked by seven hundred twelve to fifteen year olds, who were awkward to handle because of their tender age. Surging upon waves of hysteria, they were not in the least tender with the security staff or police:

> En masse they were a frightening sight. We had to seek help from the Metropolitan Police, who waged a long battle to control them in Langham Street. The difficulty was that you cannot man-handle kids. Therefore it was an unfair battle. One policeman sustained a broken arm. Another, who became trapped in the heavy swing doors, finished up with broken ribs. It took some time to release him from underneath the screaming kids, who had trampled on him.

'The worst pop group ever to enter Broadcasting House were the Sex Pistols,' says Phil:

> They behaved worse than animals, spitting and swearing all over the place. They were so obnoxious that Programme Staff virtually refused to work with them. Fortunately that type of 'performer' disappeared very quickly.
>
> There is a charisma about Broadcasting House that people pick up once they step aboard. Much of the Reithian era still exists because there are still literally hundreds dedicated to the job of broadcasting, who don't worry about stopping and starting times.

In December, Phil is responsible for buying Christmas trees. He didn't like those supplied by contractors, so took it upon himself to acquire them.

> Last year (1985) I purchased five. One conifer, I decorated red, white and blue, especially for Radio One. This inspired Terry Wogan to say in his early-morning Radio Two programme that there was a display of red, white and blue flowers on the roof-garden. A few days afterwards, a delightful old couple, who had journeyed up from Devon

came aboard to ask if they might see the flowers that Terry had described.

Unfortunately we had to tell them that there were no such flowers; that Terry wasn't telling the truth because he couldn't even see the roof garden from his studio!

Phil also had more difficult problems:

Occasionally we get mentally disturbed people coming in asking to see the Chairman or the Director-General. When the receptionists are satisfied that they are not genuine appointments they come to inform me. I then meet them, posing as the Chairman, the DG or the Head of Programme Correspondence. Eventually the Chairman, Stuart Young, discovered I was doing this. He asked me if impersonating him was difficult. I said of course it was because, unlike me, he was a young man, good-looking and slim.

I used to convince these uncertain callers by saying as the Chairman of the BBC, I would do whatever I could for them. They used to depart quite happily really believing that they had spoken to the Chairman himself.

Leaving Phil to his duties, which now included the dispersal of twenty-five cleaners to various offices and the supervision of super-porters, who moved furniture and cleaned studios, I descended to the bowels of the ship.

In the boiler-room, Edward William Teagle, Maintenance Fitter in charge of boilers and diesels in the Power House, had already started his daily routine work of boiler testing. This involved blowing down side valves, inspecting the alarm system and checking the temperature. The five boilers provide 10,000 lb of steam per hour. The original ship-like boilers were removed in 1968. There are now three fuel boilers and two gas.

'Have you ever had a crisis in your twenty-seven years service?' I asked Ted.

'Only once,' he replied, 'when a power failure lost us the shipping forecast.'

Passing the generators that drive the lifts, I remembered one vintage broadcaster, still appearing on programmes today, who rose to dizzy heights in Broadcasting House some time before he became a professional actor. Maurice Denham was apprenticed to Waygood-Otis, the firm that installed the original elevators in BH:

> I was responsible for servicing those lifts. I had to straddle the girders on top of them to be winched gradually up to the eighth floor. I had large tins of grease, which I poured into the cups and poles on either side of the elevators as we slowly descended down the eleven floors. There were no indicators in those lifts. The floor numbers were housed in a little toy cage, attached to a piece of cat-gut. The cat-gut stretched badly, so I had to tie knots in it.

After his training with the Toc H Drama League, then later with the Hull Repertory Company, in March 1938, Maurice Denham came to Broadcasting House to act in a documentary programme called 'History of Flight'.

It was in ITMA ('It's That Man Again') that he made his name as a broadcaster in 1939–40 playing in 'drag' Tommy Handley's first landlady, Mrs Lola Tickle, who was eventually replaced by Mrs Mopp.

After war service, in November 1945, he joined Kenneth Horne, Richard Murdoch and Sam Costa, playing the eccentric Dudley Davenport and other characters in 'Much Binding in the Marsh'.

By this time, the lifts were filling up with staff on their way to offices and studios to prepare the daily programmes.

Although dress is far more informal nowadays, there are still many, notably a bunch of devoted lady secretaries, who dress conservatively, valuing the old traditions of smart appearance and good taste that existed in Reith's day. Clothes worn by the younger generations tend to vary considerably especially during weekends, when the atmosphere is more relaxed. One may see men in tee-shirts or blouses, girls in jeans or trousers, even Bermuda shorts have been seen.

The House Foremen under Phil Scott are provided with

clerical grey suits, a tie and a badge. The Commissionaires have white tops to their caps. The recently refurbished entrance hall they guard was described by the late Chairman, George Howard, as having 'a museum look with glass cases'. He had hoped to bring it back to the style of the 1930s.

It is remarkable that for almost the entire period of fifty-five years that Broadcasting House has been in operation, there have been only four Heads of Drama: Val Gielgud, who served in this role for thirty-two years, Martin Esslin for thirteen, Ronald Mason (who retired in the autumn of 1986) for ten years, and John Tydeman.

In his fifth-floor office, Ronald Mason revealed to me that the current rate for broadcasting a one-hour play on radio is £4,000; that 'Saturday Night Theatre' still has an audience of over one million; that it would take ten years for an Agatha Christie play running in London's West End to match the audience of 'Saturday Night Theatre' plus its repeat; that the average audience listening to 'The Afternoon Play' (Radio 4) would fill the National Theatre for a whole year.

Annually, ten thousand plays are submitted by budding playwrights. Among those who enjoyed the experience of writing radio plays were that prolific author Tom Stoppard, and Sue Townsend, responsible for the recent success *The Diary of Adrian Mole*.

Later in the morning, I called upon the man responsible for Radio Four Planning and Presentation, Jim Black, who oversees the Announcers on this network.

Although he started his BBC career in the Regions – he was Studio Manager in Manchester and a Talks and Current Affairs Producer in Leeds – he always felt destined to work in Broadcasting House:

I used to come down to London on special rate coach journeys as a lad of eleven. I visited the studios, talked to the Commissionaires and attended all the audience shows. My first impression of Broadcasting House was that it was a place of mystery, intrigue and opportunities. It is a pity BH has become outdated. For me it has always had an aura of romance and I wish it was possible to keep the show on the road here indefinitely.

Stories about Announcers are numerous. The one I like best concerns Richard Baker, OBE, who has nightmarish memory of 'clock-stopping':

It happened when I was a Newsreader on the Home Service. As such I had to sleep overnight in BH to be on call for the early bulletins. The office where I slept had a clock, which ticked loudly every thirty seconds, unendurable if you were trying to get to sleep, so I decided to stop it.

In the secretary's desk I found a nailfile, and with this managed to unscrew something at the back of the clock, which had the desired effect. The time was ten past one.

After this I fell asleep. I woke in good time at about 5.45 a.m. with the aid of my own alarm, but when I went outside the office, I noticed that the clock at the end of the corridor registered ten past one, as did the clock in the canteen, as did the clock in the studio. In effect, I had stopped every clock in Broadcasting House!

Men with large bunches of keys had spent the entire night going round the building trying to locate the fault. I even had to ring TIM before announcing the time on the air.'

In the immediate postwar years, power cuts were a national hazard. At that time, Colin Doran was a Continuity Announcer, not yet 'fully-fledged'. Lionel Marson, who was scheduled to read the 9.00 p.m. News, had a leg disability. When all the lights went out in Broadcasting House, he was hobbling up the stairs with the aid of a stick. With two flights to go before reaching the News studio, it was obvious that he wasn't going to get there on time.

At just two minutes to the zero hour of 9.00 p.m. Colin was told that he would have to read the fifteen-minute bulletin. To make this possible, he was provided with five candles because there was no 'emergency light'.

A Radio 3 Announcer, Peter Barker, survived an equally fraught experience. Shortly before he was due to read *his* fifteen-minute bulletin, he had been familiarizing his colleagues with his hobby of making wine, when a bottle of his best vintage elderberry splintered, badly cutting his hand. 'I'm going to read the News,' he declared. 'Get me a bucket!' Peter read the News with blood steadily dripping into the bucket held by a Duty Fireman. While doing so, his face assumed a paler and paler hue.

Before Radio Two started to operate a twenty-four-hour service, the early morning Continuity Announcer was responsible for opening up the Network at 5.30 a.m. For a while, this duty befell John Dunn. Like Richard Baker, he had to sleep in BH but one morning his alarm did not ring. In the nick of time, he sprinted down to the studio to start the day's programmes. After finishing his particular programme and handing over to the next Presenter, John got into a lift, which he thought would return him to the seclusion of his sleeping quarters which he had evacuated so suddenly. Unfortunately the lift went down instead of up.

'I thought I would return to my room unobserved, that I had the whole building to myself. To my great embarrassment, the lift doors opened on the ground floor and the whole of Broadcasting House got in. Everyone had arrived for work to see me standing there bare-footed in my pyjamas!'

That very week, the famous Langham Hotel, which opened in 1865, and had been occupied by the BBC since the early days of the Second World War, was being evacuated to be sold. For nearly half a century, it had housed many production offices, conference rooms, bedrooms and the BBC Club. Many veteran broadcasters were paying a farewell visit to this sprawling Gothic landmark, which the revered architectual journalist, Sir Nikolaus Pevsner once described as 'a Victorian monster'.

The first Club member I encountered was the pianist, Dennis Gomm, whose maiden broadcast from BH was with the Olaf Sextet on 22 May 1932 from Studio BA. It was a 'live' broadcast to the Empire at 2.00 a.m. 'Broadcasting House impressed me,' said Dennis, 'as being a superior place, an elegant place. I particularly liked the flowers that were arranged in tiny alcoves. No smoking was allowed in the studios. If one lit up a cigarette, a fireman would appear within twenty seconds.'

When he was at school, Dennis Gomm's parents paid 6d a time for him to take piano lessons in Tooting. In 1925, his father, a violinist, was approached by a local cinema manager, who asked him: 'Could your boy play for the pictures?' 'Certainly, give him a trial!' Dennis was taken on at a wage of £1 per week plus five shillings for wardrobe. He remembers:

> I was sent the synopsis of each film for which I had to play. I played three and a half minutes for love scenes and two and a half minutes for Villain themes.
>
> When the first talking picture, Al Jolson's *The Singing Fool* arrived, it heralded disaster for us musicians. In those days big cinemas had orchestras with as many as eighty players. Thousands were thrown out of work throughout the whole country, because naturally the special cinema music we played to accompany silent films became worthless after the advent of sound.'

Later, at Broadcasting House, Dennis played with the BBC Variety Orchestra. He arranged the signature tune, a waltz, 'Roses from the South', for the Grand Hotel programme featuring the Winter Garden Orchestra. The title 'Winter Garden' was later changed to 'Palm Court', and he continued to play with this popular orchestra for many years.

I shared a snack in the lounge restaurant with David Jacobs, who had just finished his daily lunchtime programme. He nostalgically remembered the long-running detective serial 'Dick Barton, Special Agent': 'I was an avid listener, never actually played the role, but when I came out of Broadcasting House one evening, the assembled crowd seemed convinced I was the Special Agent himself. Not wishing to disappoint them, I signed all their autograph books: "Dick Barton".'

Next, I met Duncan Carse, who as off-duty Overseas Presentation Assistant was so active in saving lives in Broadcasting House on the 'night of the bomb' in 1940 and later served in the Royal Navy. He succeeded Noel Johnson as Dick

Barton in January 1949.

News Reporters revealed that this six-foot-tall, thirty-eight-year-old broadcaster had been sea-going and exploring since the age of nineteen; that he had served in the Royal Research Ship *Discovery II* on a thirteen-month voyage, later spending two years with the British Graham Land expedition. Duncan holds the rare Polar Medal for his Antarctic explorations.

'I remember when joining the BBC as an Announcer,' said Duncan, 'my first encounter with Stuart Hibberd. He was a man of immense kindness. His opening words to me were: "Have an apple!" He found a pippin for me in his briefcase.'

There was serious training for Announcers conducted by an expert in spoken English, Commander E.J. King-Bull, who was brilliant at analyzing the technique of announcing. He used to put everyone through their paces, actors and actresses as well. When he introduced himself to one actress as King-Bull, recalled Duncan, her flippant reply was: 'I'm Queen Cow.'

Many programme staff take a 'working' lunch. For this they largely rely on a trolley service attractively supervised with a joyful word and a smile from a dark-haired lady from Edmonton, known to everyone in BH as Joyce. Joyce Sylvia Rose started work in Broadcasting House as a table cleaner. After working for three and a half years in the restaurant, she started her own trolley service, which she has been running for twenty-five years. From her trolley, still clanging along in the late nineteen-eighties, she serves cups of tea at 6p per cup, hot chocolate and coffee at 11p, sandwiches from 21p to 56p and salads at a few pence more.

At morning coffee time 9p doughnuts made on the premises are firm favourites. It was these sugar-coated, jam-filled delicacies that caught the eye of the Prime Minister, the Rt. Hon. Margaret Thatcher, on her way to an interview with Jimmy Young. In passing, she told Joyce that she fancied one. It being a busy time, Joyce said with her disarming smile: 'You'll have to join the queue, Madam.'

One Christmas Eve, Joyce was serving afternoon tea from her trolley, parked outside the Studio Manager's office. One of her customers asked her if she had any cigars.

'No,' said Joyce, 'but I can get you some from the restaurant. Hold on!'

She returned with the cigars to find that her trolley was missing. She soon discovered it inside the Studio Manager's office, festooned with streamers, holly and mistletoe.

Favourite stars Joyce has served from her trolley include Charlton Heston, Howard Keel, and more recently Dak Rambo from 'Dallas'. She says:

Some of my regulars tell me their worries and troubles, even invite me to their weddings. One was in Berkeley Square. I love working in Broadcasting House, the people I meet. I would never want to work anywhere else. This spring, at Easter, I got the surprise of my life. Gloria Hunniford was scheduled to do interviews for her afternoon programme at the Ritz Hotel in Piccadilly, and what do you think? My Catering Manageress, Gillian Black-Campbell, kindly arranged for me to go along with her. It was really wonderful. I felt like Cinderella at the Ball with Gloria as my Fairy Godmother.

All ships are subject to periodic repairs. HMS Broadcasting House is no exception. For six consecutive years, from 1974 to 1980, a thirty-five-foot crack in the 'prow' underwent restoration. The crack was caused by an unprotected rusting steel frame. Over the years, water seeping through minute cracks gradually started corrosion, causing the rusting steel to move the Portland stone cladding. Stonemasons were contracted to strip the steel beam of rust, treat it and encase it in concrete before re-assembling the stone work. Scaffolding was erected between the fifth and eighth floors. The vibrating noises from the drilling and hammering were disturbing for crews occupying offices for Radio 4 Current Affairs programmes, including 'Farming To-day'.

Lattice masts have remained on the roof since 1932. The uninitiated might well be forgiven for imagining that all BBC programmes radiated from them. The one above the clock is merely a decoration, whereas the two for'ard ones have supported aerials though they were never used for broadcasting. These too eventually became victims of the corrosive atmosphere and were removed by crane for maintenance. They were pickled, galvanized and returned to the Upper Deck as good as new.

After a quick 'cuppa' from Joyce's trolley, I descended to the Half Deck to keep an appointment with the then Director-General, Alisdair Milne, in the Captain's oak-panelled cabin. He told me:

Sadly, Broadcasting House, so long the heart of the operation has become obsolete. It is no longer a place in which to do modern radio. In the first part of the next decade crews will be moving into a new purpose-built Broadcasting Centre at the White City. We couldn't remain here much longer, patching up and replacing antiquated equipment.

Another problem has been that since Marmaduke Tudsbery had the task of avoiding the Bakerloo Tube, the rattle of the subway trains has been increased by the introduction of two more Underground lines. Owing to the noise and vibrations, one of the Drama Studies has become virtually untenable.

Broadcasting House has kept wonderful traditions, but now even the Boardroom is not big enough for all the Board to assemble there together.

The new Centre will be tremendously exciting with superb acoustics and conditions to match. A new era will begin.

I shook the skipper by the hand, walked along the deep-piled carpet past the Boardroom, where hang the portrait photographs of all previous Chairmen, and the Council Chamber, whose walls are adorned with oil paintings of past Director-Generals.

I was harbouring mixed feelings about the new horizon. HMS Broadcasting House and its crews had become an integral part of my life. A listed building since 1981, the flagship will proudly remain at her berth in Portland Place to give 'back-up' services to the new Centre. It will be a splendid 'museum-piece', perhaps to be happily visited in the future by lovers of steam radio just as long as Nation continues to speak Peace unto Nation.

I descended in Maurice Denham's lift to the Main Entrance Hall, then walked slowly past the two Commissionaires, through the heavy doors, out into the late afternoon sunlight under the shadows of Prospero and Ariel.

END OF VOYAGE

Index